The Colson Center Presents

THE IMAGE RESTORED

THE IMAGO DEI AND CREATION

GLENN SUNSHINE

TIMOTHY D. PADGETT

INTRODUCTION BY JOHN STONESTREET

COLSON PRESS

The Image Restored: The Image of God and Creation

Copyright © 2021 The Colson Center for Christian Worldview

The Colson Center, P.O. Box 62160 Colorado Springs, CO 80962

All rights reserved. Brief quotations of this material is permitted, but contact The Colson Center regarding permission for longer selections.

The Colson Center Editorial Team:
Isaac Hans, Timothy D. Padgett, Brian Brown, and Elena Sorensen

Table of Contents

The Image of God and...

Introduction	6
1. Stewardship	12
2. Human Dignity	22
3. Gender	33
4. Marriage	42
5. Spirituality	52
6. Creativity	61
7. Reason	70
8. Work	80
9. Science	89
10. Freedom	97
11. The Fall	106
12. Jesus the Christ	115
13. Restoration	123
14. The Cultural Mandate	131

Introduction

by John Stonestreet

In his book *A Brief History of Thought*, atheist philosopher Luc Ferry described Christianity's unique contribution to Western culture: "Christianity was to introduce the notion that humanity was fundamentally identical, that men were equal in dignity, an unprecedented idea at the time, and one to which our world owes its entire democratic inheritance."

This vision of what it means to be human is, Ferry suggested, the only historical grounding for concepts now taken for granted as essential to a flourishing society, such as dignity and human value. Ferry then writes, "But this notion of equality didn't come from nowhere." Specifically, it was the idea of the imago dei, that every human person bears the image of God, that has proven among the most consequential in human history. Even more, it is an idea essential for both a grounded Christian worldview and an effectual Christian witness.

Two things are at the root of our culture-wide confusion about what it means to be human. First, our culture has forgotten what it means to be human because our culture has forgotten God. Second, the church has neglected to catechize its own about this essential idea. While most Christians would know *that* every single person is made in the image of God, very few could articulate or explain *what it means* to bear God's image, how the world is different because of the imago dei within it, and the implications of the imago dei for the various layers of society.

There are, theologically speaking, three ways of thinking about the imago dei. The first approach emphasizes the functional aspects of humanity. That is, humans are in the image of God because they are able to do the kinds of things that God does: God creates; humans create. God is rational; humans are rational. God speaks; humans speak. Of course, if a particular image bearer loses, by injury or accident, abilities unique to human beings, they've not lost the image itself. So, there must remain distinction between what we can do and who we are.

The second approach emphasizes the relational aspects of humanity. We bear the image of God who is Father, Son, and Holy Spirit. Within a Christian worldview, God doesn't do relationships, He is a relationship in His very essence. There's much to ponder here.

The third approach, and the one most clearly seen in those Biblical texts that describe the creation of humanity by God, emphasizes the status or place of humanity within the created order. By explaining the sort of role that we play in the world, the Scriptures tells us what humans are for.

Consider Genesis 1:26-28:

> Then God said, "Let us make mankind in our image, in our likeness, so that they may rule over the fish in the sea and the birds in the sky, over the livestock and all the wild animals, and over all the creatures that move along the ground." So God created mankind in his own image, in the image of God he created them; male and female he created them. God blessed them and said to them, "Be fruitful and increase in number; fill the earth and subdue it. Rule over the fish in the sea and the birds in the sky and over every living creature that moves on the ground." (NIV)

The fundamental assumption up to this point within the creation narrative is the fundamental theological assumption throughout all of the Scriptures: God is the Ruler of the cosmos. He is the Sovereign. The creation is His. It exists at His command.

And yet, in the concluding description of the creation week quoted above, the absolute Ruler creates others who will rule. In fact, the first people who would hear of this jaw-dropping moment of Creation would be the chosen people, the Israelites, newly free from Egyptian slavery. The contrast they must have sensed then, from the slaves they were to the rulers they are, should be enough to spark our imaginations today.

In fact, there's an ordering to what God needed His people to learn in the creation narrative. He had already given them a new theology and a new cosmology. In contrast to what they had heard in Egypt, that there were many gods each claiming sovereignty over particular aspects of creation, God made clear He is the only One and nothing is outside of His rule.

Here, God has given them a new anthropology. He tells these erstwhile slaves that their true role is to "rule over the fish of the sea and the birds of the air, over the livestock, over all the earth, and over all creatures that move along the ground." In this beautiful, poetic way, they learn humanity has been put in charge of everything else God created.

They are not autonomous, to be clear. They are not to rule by their own standards. They are God's representatives, and are to rule God's world according to God's purposes for God's glory. This is what humans are for. Humans play the most significant role in the creation story other than God Himself.

How were they to rule? Look back at verse 28: "God blessed them and said to them, 'Be fruitful and increase in number. Fill the earth and subdue it.'"

In Genesis 1:2, we read that the Earth was formless and void. The rest of the chapter until the creation of humanity describes how God, in response, filled and formed what was empty and formless. He now gives this task to His image bearers. They are to fill the Earth and subdue it (in the sense of subduing a garden, not a cockroach).

Like the God whose image we bear, humans are to make something of the world. We are to make the world bigger, better, and fuller. In fact, though God places Adam and Eve in a beautiful Garden, He did not wish for them to stay there. They are to be fruitful and multiply, to fill the earth. In a sense, they were to turn all of the earth into a garden. As God fills and forms and rules, so too, humanity reflects His image by our own work in this world.

The fundamental truth here is that every single human being has a given identity. They bear the image and likeness of God. This identity establishes for every single human being both dignity and value. To say that we are not created in the image of God, or that there is no God who shares His image, or that our identity as human beings somehow lies in something other than the imago dei is to untether human dignity from the only thing that has ever grounded it. Anytime human dignity is severed from the image of God, some people are left out, which is the central fact of so many of the horrors we've seen in human history.

To hold the Biblical story together and to see the imago dei within that story is to realize something crucial for truly knowing who we are. Christ, in redemption, is after what God intended in creation. This is part of the significance the word redemption. All "Re" words, in fact, point us back: return, renew, restore, redeem, reconcile, resurrection, even repentance. In a culture that has forgotten what it means to be human, there is a Savior who intends to restore our humanness. Of all the answers offered by various worldviews and religions to the "what is humanity" question, the Christian vision of the imago Dei is the best. It is the only alternative that simultaneously grounds dignity, secures freedom, and offers moral boundaries.

We have a better story. As Chuck Colson said in his very last speech; Christians do not impose; they propose. Christians have the better answer, the better vision of reality. We have a much better answer to the question of it means to be human than any other on the market. As Thomas Howard said, "The Incarnation takes all that properly belongs to our humanity and delivers it back to us redeemed."

What if that is true? What if the best thing Christians can offer the world is redeemed humanness? What if the world around us could see this image restored?

Chapter 1

The Image of God and Stewardship

To be human

One of the most important statements in Scripture about what it means to be human occurs in the very first chapter of the Bible:

> *Then God said, "Let us make man in our image, after our likeness. And let them have dominion over the fish of the sea and over the birds of the heavens and over the livestock and over all the earth." So God made man in his own image, in the image of God he created him; male and female he created them.* (Gen. 1:26-27 ESV)

Although this is the essence of the Biblical definition of humanity, it is frequently ignored, misinterpreted, or given little real consideration by contemporary Christians. Missing this point leaves us with little practical foundation

The Image of God and Stewardship 13

for understanding the multi-faceted responsibilities God has given us in this world.

Before exploring what the image of God is, let's clear up some misconceptions that come from misunderstand the way the phrase "image of god" was used in the ancient Near East.

- The image of God is not about seeing God as a human being writ large. Some have suggested it is just an explanation for anthropomorphic deities (i.e., gods who look like humans). Aside from getting things backward—if anything, the term describes humans as "theomorphic" (God-shaped) rather than God as anthropomorphic (human-shaped)—this idea misses the point of what the phrase was trying to convey. It says nothing about God, and everything about humanity and our responsibility to God.

- The image of God is not about human beings having a body like God's. This also misses the point. Scripture is clear that God is Spirit (Jn. 4:24) and the only body He has is Jesus'. Yes, Scripture describes God as having arms, eyes, and ears, but these are metaphors to convey His ability to know and act in the world and do not tell us that God actually has a human-like body any more than the passages that say we are sheltered under His wings suggest that God is a heavenly chicken.

- The image of God is not a form of idolatry. This is the claim of Islam. Mohammed grew up in the world of Arabian paganism, where idols were everywhere. In his move to monotheism, he rightly recognized that God does not have a body and so Islam absolutely banned any images of Allah because of the fear that they would lead people back to paganism and idolatry. Like the second commandment, Islam also argues that any representation of God is by nature false, but Mohammed and his followers did not understand the significance of the phrase "image of God" in its cultural context. It does not refer to anything idolatrous. Ironically enough, its principal meaning is not very different from Islam's understanding of the place of humans in the world.

So what did the phrase "image of god" mean in the ancient Near East? To answer that, we need to know something about the history of the area. In the Mesopotamian world, life was unpredictable and precarious. The area was subject to erratic and destructive flooding and was vulnerable to invasion. It is no wonder then that the city states were literally built around religion: the center of every city was a ziggurat, a temple to the city's major deity and whose priests dominated the civilization, at least initially.

Over time, a power struggle ensued between warlords known as ensi and the priests. To legitimize their authority in these highly theocratic societies, the ensi associated themselves with the gods, claiming to be their official regents and representatives to the world. This enabled them to emerge as kings with a credible claim to rule over the priests.

These kings were commonly referred to as the images of a god; they were that god's "face" in this world and this gave them the right to rule.

Royal authority!

By designating human beings as the image of God, Genesis confers royal authority on us. This idea is further reinforced by the language in the rest of Gen. 1:26. In Hebrew, when you want to emphasize something, you repeat it. Thus, the angelic beings in Isaiah 6 and Revelation 4 declare God to be "holy, holy, holy." Similarly, Hebrew poetry is characterized by "parallelism," the repetition of an idea in different words. This can be seen in Ps.1:1-2 (ESV):

> *Blessed is the man*
> *who walks not in the counsel of the wicked,*
> *nor stands in the way of sinners*
> *nor sits in the seat of scoffers;*
> *but his delight is in the law of the LORD*
> *and on his law he meditates day and night.*

The indented lines show parallelism at work: each line in the two groups repeats and elaborates on the same basic theme.

In Gen. 1:26, for the first and only time in the creation story, God pauses and consults with Himself about something He is about to create. The pronouncement He makes highlights the fact that something special is about to occur, and as is suited to the occasion, the language is heightened by the kind of parallelism we see in Hebrew poetry. God says He is going to create humanity in His image, and then elaborates on what that means by indicating that we are to have "dominion" over fish, birds, livestock, and all the earth.

At this point, a lot of Christians get nervous, because we know from history how tyrannical royalty can be. "Dominion" easily turns into domination and abuse. And in fact, Christians have been regularly accused of using this verse as an excuse for everything from strip mining and plundering resources to pollution.

That is a fair concern, but we need to bear in mind that to abuse God's creation is to twist what this dominion actually is. We must recognize that in the ancient Near East, royal authority came from a god and thus was exercised in the god's name and under the god's authority. This is especially true in Genesis. True, we are given authority, but it is the authority of a steward, not of an independent monarch.

The Lord of the Rings (the novel more than the movie) illustrates the difference well. The stewards of Gondor have absolute authority to rule the city in the absence of the king, protecting it and holding it until such time as the king returns. The steward Denethor makes it clear to Boromir that they can never become kings, because that is not their place. If or when the king returns, the stewards are to return their stewardship to him and are to be judged for the faithfulness with which they carried out their duties. As 1 Cor. 4:2 puts it, it is required of stewards that they be found faithful.

In the same way, the earth is the Lord's, not ours (Ps. 24:1). We may have dominion, but it is only the dominion of a steward, carrying with it the responsibility to pass on a carefully tended and protected world to our heirs and to Christ when He returns.

This is not a new understanding of our environmental responsibilities. For example, John Calvin, who is regularly (and wrongly) vilified as providing the theological justification for out-of-control capitalism and the accompanying exploitation of the environment, had this to say in his commentary on Gen. 2:15:

> *Let him who possesses a field, so partake of its yearly fruits, that he may not suffer the ground to be injured by his negligence; but let him endeavour to hand it down to posterity as he received it, or even better cultivated. Let him so feed on its fruits, that he neither dissipates it by luxury, nor permits [it] to be marred or ruined by neglect. Moreover, that this economy, and this diligence with*

respect to those good things which God has given us to enjoy, may flourish among us; let every one regard himself as the steward of all things which he possesses. Then he will neither conduct himself dissolutely, nor corrupt by abuse those things which God required to be preserved.[1]

In his sermon on Gen. 2:7-15, Calvin adds that whether rich or poor, we must remember that whatever we have, we must use it with the sure knowledge that one day we will have to give an account to God of what we have done with the things He has entrusted to us.[2]

A question of stewardship

The historical Christian tradition has thus been committed to environmental stewardship, recognizing that though we have authority on Earth, we also have great responsibility to use and develop the world as caretakers of God's possession. We cannot fall into the trap of worshiping the world, as both ancient and modern paganism has done, but we cannot neglect our responsibilities either.

In the first instance, the image of God refers to humanity as royalty, appointed by God as His representatives,

---

[1] John Calvin, *Commentaries on the First Book of Moses Called Genesis*, translated from the original Latin and compared with the French edition, by the Rev. John King, vol. 1 (Edinburgh: Calvin Translation Society; reprinted Grand Rapids: Baker, 2005), 125.

[2] Jean Calvin, *Sermons sur la Genèse*, Chapitres 1,1-11,4, ed. Max Engammare (Neukirchen-Vluyn: Neukirchener Verlag, 2000), 108-109.

regents, and stewards over creation. This gives us enormous responsibilities, but also dignity and the right to enjoy the creation. It also establishes the only firm foundation for the idea of universal human rights, the subject our next chapter.

Questions

1. Read Gen. 1:26. What does it mean to you that God created humanity in His image? Have you ever given any thought to what that says about us and about God?

2. What does the concept of human beings having dominion over the world mean to you? Do you see this as a positive or a negative?

3. In 1967, historian Lynn White, Jr., wrote an essay entitled "The Historical Roots of Our Ecological Crisis." This essay argued that the Bible's teaching on human dominion was responsible for the environmental degradation that was a growing concern in the 1960s. This argument has now become a staple of the environmental movement. Without getting into the historical arguments, do you think the Bible teaches a kind of dominion that can lead to environmental degradation and abuse? Why or why not?

4. Read Lev. 25:23, Deut. 10:14, Ps. 24:1, and Job 41:11. What do these verses add to your understanding of the nature of humanity's dominion over the Earth?

5. Stewardship is defined in the Holman Bible Dictionary (1991) as "utilizing and managing all resources God provides for the glory of God and the betterment of His creation." Do you think this definition successfully balances God's authority and humanity's dominion? Why or why not?

6. What resources (e.g., time, talent, treasure, truth, relationships) has God entrusted to your stewardship? How are you handling your stewardship of them? Which areas do you need to pay more attention to?

EXTRA THOUGHTS
By Timothy D. Padgett

Christians like to talk a lot about the concept of human dignity, and generally the conversation shifts quickly to the question of the image of God. This happens for good reason. Unlike the reigning paradigms of our postmodern age, Christianity, with its emphasis on the doctrine of the Imago Dei, offers the world a solution to a pressing problem. How do we judge the value of our fellow man? With its naturalistic presupposition, our society can provide no explanation of personal value apart from external traits like what we can do and whether we belong to the "right" group.

In Christianity, our value is in our essence, not our effort. Human beings are created with a dignity conferred by God Himself. Dignity is not a side effect of abilities or ethnicity. It is an honor which we do not earn, nor is it judged by others, but is attached to our very nature. Human dignity is not the sole property of the strong, the healthy, the wealthy, or the powerful. It belongs in equal measure to the weak, the sick, the handicapped, and the unborn.

Chapter 2

The Image of God and Human Dignity

God's representative

In the first chapter, we saw that the phrase "image of God" was a royal term that described humanity as the official representative and regent of God in this world. This leads to the biblical teaching of human dominion over nature, but at the same time limits the terms of that dominion to acting as God's steward in the world and taking care of it appropriately as His possession.

Since in Genesis 1 the description of humanity focuses entirely on the image of God, it follows that this is the most essential element of what it means to be human. This then has implications well beyond dominion and stewardship. In particular, it provides the only real foundation for human dignity and human rights.

Dignified above all else

First, the image of God distinguishes us from everything else in creation. Spain may grant "human rights" to great apes[1] and Switzerland may have enshrined plant rights into their constitution,[2] but neither of these alter the fundamental distinction between humans and either animals or plants. In fact, they demonstrate the difference: has any other species given rights to anything else? Has any other species acted to protect other species? Has any other species held itself in check in an effort to prevent another species from extinction?

The very fact that we can talk about rights and that we recognize our responsibilities toward other creatures puts the lie to the claims of animal rights activists that we are just another species on the planet, no different from any other. If that's the case, why do they insist that we must protect and respect other species? If they don't ask that of termites in a house, which destroy our habitat, or a lion meeting a lone wildebeest, why do they expect it of humans? Or should we put predatory animals in jail?

We do in fact have responsibilities to other creatures, and for that reason the animal and plant rights activists who deny a special place for humans are wrong. It is precisely

---

[1] http://www.guardian.co.uk/world/2008/jun/26/humanrights.animalwelfare.
[2] http://www.weeklystandard.com/Content/Public/Articles/000/000/015/065njdoe.asp.

our creation in the image of God that gives us those responsibilities and that distinguishes us from the rest of Creation. The claim that this outlook is "speciesism," a moral failing akin to racism, is self-refuting unless those leveling the charge are also willing to say that all other species have the same responsibilities—not just rights—that we do.

Christians have supported an appropriate form of animal rights for centuries. For example, William Wilberforce, the British evangelical who led the fight in Parliament against the slave trade, also was a founder of the Royal Society for the Prevention of Cruelty to Animals. But equating animal rights to human rights is a different issue altogether, and points to a fundamental deterioration in our culture's understanding of, and commitment to, the value of human dignity, and with it to human life itself.

The image of God and the value of life

In biblical terms, humanity's unique dignity flows from our creation in God's image. Since we are God's regents on the earth, an attack on any human being is tantamount to an attack on God Himself. Thus, God tells Noah after the flood:

> *Whoever sheds the blood of man,*
> *by man shall his blood be shed,*
> *for God made man in his own image.* (Gen. 9:6 ESV)

The justification in this instance for capital punishment was the fact that human beings are made in God's image. Murderers forfeited their right because of their attack on one of God's image bearers. That is how seriously God takes human life.

Taking this one step further, since the value of human life flows from the image of God, so does human dignity. And since the image of God is shared by all people, all of us have an intrinsic dignity that is distinct from anything else about us. *The supreme value of the image of God far outweighs any other consideration in determining our worth.*

Insulting God?

To put it simply, any time you value something more than the image of God in how you think about yourself or others—whether race, sex, class, appearance, age, mental capacity, ability, disability, anything—you are quite literally insulting God to His face.

This includes valuing people on the basis of their religious beliefs. Christians who think they are better than others because of their faith have forgotten a fundamental element of the gospel. We are all sinners who can bring nothing good to God that would make us worthy of salvation. But what we could not provide for ourselves, God provided for us. The fact that we are Christians says more about the mercy and grace of God than it does about us. Christians thus have no claim to being better than anyone else, and we must insist that all human beings are equally valuable regardless of faith, lifestyle, vices, criminal background, or anything else, because we all share the image of God.

There is therefore never any excuse for any form of bigotry, whether racism, sexism, classism, ageism, ableism, or any of the other "-isms" of our culture. As a result, Christians should be (and historically have been) at the forefront of fights for civil rights.

The image of God and human equality

From its earliest days, Christianity has argued for human equality before God. The apostle Paul tells us that in Christ, "there is neither Jew nor Greek, there is neither slave nor free, there is neither male nor female." (Gal. 3:28 ESV) All are morally and spiritually equal before God, all equally need salvation, and all share in the same means of salvation. Race, class and gender thus are irrelevant before God.

This emphasis on moral and spiritual equality led Christians to be the first people anywhere in the world to pass laws against slavery.[3] Slavery was condemned as a sin in Thomas Aquinas's Summa Theologica, and when the Europeans tapped into the African slave trade, no fewer than four

---

[3] Rodney Stark, Victory of Reason, 29-31

popes condemned it.[4] And of course, the British abolition campaign in the late eighteenth century was led by evangelical Christians, among them William Wilberforce.

Martin Luther King, Jr.'s leadership in the civil rights movement was based on a profound understanding of Christian natural law theory going back at least as far as Thomas Aquinas in the early thirteenth century. King's *Letter from Birmingham Jail* is based on just these arguments, anchored in the Christian tradition that recognized both our equality and intrinsic dignity and the importance of an objective moral foundation for law.

Early Christians promoted the rights of children and the unborn as well. In an era in which infanticide was mandated by law for the handicapped and allowed under any circumstances, Christians saved babies from death, bringing them into their own households, and petitioned the government to end this legalized murder. Similarly, following the lead of the Jews, they also opposed abortion as murder since it was the taking of a human life made in the image of God.

Christians pioneered rights for women as well. As a result of converting to Christianity, women in ancient Rome gained freedom, prestige, and opportunity well beyond what was

---

[4] Ibid., 200-202.

available to them in the pagan world.[5] We will return to this topic in a later chapter.

When it comes to issues of human dignity, Christians often divide themselves into two camps, with political conservatives taking up the banner when it comes to abortion, infanticide, and euthanasia while political progressives lead the charge on questions of poverty relief and racial and gender discrimination. Both sides tragically miss something key about the image of God.

The only foundation for securing true justice in all of these cases is found in the divine imprint on every human being. This means that the prolife activist campaigning for the humanity of the unborn should for the same reason be passionate about treating women considering abortion with honor since they, too, bear the image of God. Likewise, the community organizer, working for the well-being of the poor in our midst, for the very same virtues, may be in the forefront against calls for "death with dignity."

Ultimately, the logic of our creation in the image of God led to the development of the idea of universal human rights. This is a uniquely western concept, built on theories of unalienable rights developed by medieval Christian theologians from their studies of the Bible. And it is all founded on the spiritual and moral equality of people in

---

[5] Rodney Stark, *The Rise of Christianity*, 95-128.

Christ, going back, ultimately, to our creation in the image of God.

No other culture, religion, or civilization has advanced a comparable idea, because none have a worldview foundation for it. Even Jürgen Habermas, the leading public intellectual in Europe (and an atheist), points out that modern secular ideas of human rights have their origins in the Judeo-Christian tradition, and though secularists can appropriate these ideas, denying their foundation is intellectually dishonest:

> *Egalitarian universalism, from which sprang the ideas of freedom and social solidarity, of an autonomous conduct of life and emancipation, of the individual morality of conscience, human rights and democracy, is the direct heir of the Judaic ethic of justice and the Christian ethic of love. This legacy, substantially unchanged, has been the object of continual critical appropriation and reinterpretation. To this day, there is no alternative to it. And in light of the current challenges of a postnational constellation, we continue to draw on the substance of this heritage. Everything else is just idle postmodern talk.*[6]

In an era of easy abortion coupled with ultrasounds and genetic testing to determine if the child is worth keeping alive, of designer babies, of calls for legalized euthanasia,

---

[6] *Time of Transitions*, 150.

and a host of other challenges to human life and worth in our culture, we Christians need to rediscover and recommit to the centrality of the image of God for determining human value.

Questions

1. Read Ps. 8. What does it tell you about human dignity?

2. What is the basis of your self-image? How does the fact that you were created in God's image factor into it?

3. How does our responsibility as God's stewards in the world affect our ideas of animal and plant rights? How do those rights differ from our rights as image-bearers of God?

4. Read Gal. 3:38 and Col. 3:11. What do these verses tell us about human equality before God?

5. Are there any groups in which you have a hard time seeing the image of God? Are there any groups that you see as more valuable than others? How should our common creation in the image of God affect how you think about these groups?

6. We live in a world where rape, torture, genocide, and murder happen. How do we reconcile the idea that even the people who do such things are created in the image of God, with the demands of justice and our very natural revulsion for their actions?

7. What is the connection between the image of God and human rights? Medieval theologians found unalienable rights in Scripture. Can you think of any biblical passages that support the idea of human rights in general or specific rights?

EXTRA THOUGHTS
By Timothy D. Padgett

Stewardship is one of the most obvious implications of our being made in the image of God. After all, it is right there in the first chapter of Genesis: we are to rule and hold dominion as an act of service to our Creator. At the same time, this is a concept that we in the postmodern West have great trouble grasping. We put so much emphasis on crafting our identities that we cannot fathom that our path could be assigned by another.

Stewardship is the concept that our labors and lives find purpose in fealty to a higher power. We are not our own, but we are not nothing. We are not simply animals, much less the sum of a host of chemical reactions. And we are not free agents, at liberty to act as we wish. We are agents of the creator of the universe. We have real and true authority over the natural world, but it is not ours to do with what we will. Stewardship grants us the dignity of responsibility. We have been chosen and designed to continue the artistry of the great Artist.

Chapter 3

The Image of God and Gender

From the beginning

In our first two chapters, we have seen that the image of God refers to humanity's dominion over the world as God's stewards, and that it is the basis for the unique dignity of human beings, for equality, and for human rights. In this article, we will look more closely at the issue of gender.

Gender is specifically mentioned in the first passage in Scripture dealing with the image of God: ... *God created man in his own image, in the image of God he created him; male and female he created them.* (Gen. 1:28 ESV)

Notice that the text very pointedly identifies the image of God with *both* male and female. Men and women are thus equally image bearers of God, and this means that they are intrinsically equal in worth, in their rights, and in their call to exercise dominion in God's name over the earth.

It is impossible to overstate how revolutionary this idea was in the ancient world. We sometimes hear the argument that paganism is far better for women than monotheism, because in paganism there are goddesses along with gods, thus providing women with a claim to status and even authority in society. This argument is great in theory; in practice it's total nonsense.

Women under paganism

In reality, paganism almost inevitably placed rigid restrictions on women's roles. Essentially, they were only permitted to do things that the goddesses did. And this meant that they were responsible for the domestic sphere and often little else.

In Greece, for example, "free" women did not leave the home even to go shopping—that was handled by the men or by slaves. In places like Ephesus or Corinth that were dominated by temples to goddesses, the priestesses had more public roles, but they also doubled as prostitutes. And in general, only a small number of wealthy women, priestesses, and prostitutes had any roles or responsibilities in public life.

Further, women were considered intrinsically inferior to men in almost all ancient cultures. Aristotle, for example, considered women to be essentially the result of birth defects—they were "misbegotten men," incomplete and inferior physically, morally, and intellectually.

Women also were not valued as highly as men, an attitude that persists in many parts of the world today. In Rome, wives came in a distant third for their husbands, behind parents and sons. As for children, Romans typically kept all healthy boys and their first daughter; the rest were discarded and left to die.

These problems were not limited to the Greco-Roman world. All major civilizations in the ancient world and the majority of minor cultures held women as distinctly inferior to men, with far fewer rights, privileges, or opportunities.

Judaism

Things were quite a bit different in Judaism, largely due to Genesis 1:28. Women were equal to but different from men because of their common creation in the image of God.

Spiritually, women set the tone for the entire family, so much so that it was believed that a pious man who married an evil woman would become evil, and an evil man who married a pious woman would become pious. Women were seen as than men, and some scholars argued that the wives of the patriarchs were superior to their more intuitive husbands as prophets.

Women were also highly respected. The Ten Commandments say to "Honor your father and your mother" in Ex. 20:12, but to "Honor your mother and your father" in Lev. 19:3. The fact that father comes first in one case, but mother in the other, was taken to mean parents are accorded honor equally.

Although women's primary role was as the mother and keeper of the household, they were not limited to the domestic sphere. Women had the right to own, buy and sell property and to engage in business, following the example of Proverbs 31. They also had more rights with respect to marriage than in most other cultures. Under no circumstances could husbands beat or abuse their wives.

To be sure, the Talmud says some negative things about women, with some rabbis describing them as being lazy, gluttonous, gossips, and prone to witchcraft; of course, they also describe men as being prone to lust and sexual sin. Overall, though, there can be no serious question that Jewish women were far more highly regarded and better off than their pagan neighbors, stereotypes to the contrary notwithstanding.

Christianity

Christianity carried on this tradition of honoring women. Women played important supporting roles in Jesus' ministry and were the first witnesses of the resurrection.

The Image of God and Gender

Spiritually, the distinction between men and women is erased in Christ (Gal. 3:28). Women converted to Christianity in large numbers, in part because of the respect and freedom it gave them. Some women even became leaders in the early church, sponsoring churches in their homes (e.g., Col. 4:15) and serving as deacons[1] and prophets (e.g., Acts 21:9).

Women continued to play important roles in the church into the Middle Ages and beyond, including powerful and influential abbesses who ran women's convents and sometimes double monasteries (that is, two monasteries close together, one for men and one for women), founders of religious orders such as Clare of Assisi, mystics and visionaries such as Hildegard von Bingen and Teresa of Ávila, and in the modern world highly respected religious leaders such as Mother Teresa.

Christian ethical standards also raised the status of women. Husbands were commanded to love and take care of their wives as Christ loved and took care of the church (Eph. 5:25), an unheard-of idea in the Greco-Roman world. The impact of Christianity on family life is important enough to deserve its own study, so we will return to that topic in the next chapter. For now, suffice it to say that here again,

---

[1] In addition to Phoebe (Rom. 16:1), the Roman writer Pliny the Younger wrote a letter to the Emperor Trajan asking him how to handle Christians and noting that he had arrested two female slaves who were deaconesses.

Christianity markedly improved the marital conditions for women compared to the pagan world.

Christians also joined the Jews in rejecting abortion and infanticide but went further in rescuing abandoned babies—mostly girls—and raising them in their own households.

At the same time, it must be said that the Church has not always been true to its foundations in its treatment of women. A great deal of the problem here comes from the influence of Greek misogyny on early Christian writers, who imported negative ideas about women from Aristotle, from Neo-Platonists, and from other pagan sources. It certainly does not originate from the Biblical concept of men's and women's shared creation in the image of God, nor from Jewish theory or practice.

Despite stereotypes to the contrary, Judaism and Christianity have had a more positive impact on women than any other movement in history. The image of God in both male and female was the foundation for women's rights and the ultimate source for modern ideas of gender equality. Scripture affirms that though men and women are different, they are equally valuable before God, equally worthy of honor and respect, and spiritually and morally equal in Christ.

Questions

1. Read Proverbs 31. What does this passage tell you about Israelite ideals of the role of women in the family and society?

2. Where do you see women's rights and status under attack in the world today? In what ways do you see practices similar to those of the ancient world? What should be our response to these attacks?

3. Think about the views of women that are common in our culture today. In what ways do they correspond with the teachings of the Bible? In what ways do they depart from the Bible?

4. Why do you think it is important to understand the role of Judaism and Christianity in the development of women's rights throughout history?

5. Using what you now know, how would you respond to someone who claims that Christianity is oppressive to women?

6. How do you reconcile the Bible's affirmation of differences between the genders with the Bible's insistence that men and women are equal image bearers of God? How does this play out in families, churches, and society?

EXTRA THOUGHTS
By Brooke B. McIntire, Content Manager, What Would You Say?

In our attempts to rectify any treatment of women as inferior, we champion the cause of "Equality!" But in our enthusiasm, we are in danger of mistaking "equality" for "sameness." God is a masterful designer, capable of making beings equal in value, dignity, and purpose without making them the same. In fact, our differences as male and female allow us to reflect the relational and life-giving aspects of God's nature.

Did you know that the root word "gen" – as in genesis, generation, or gender – means "that which produces"? The difference between the genders is the way in which they are designed to produce new life. This is obviously seen in biological reality (you need both genders to produce a biological life), but unity and cooperation of the genders fosters life in relational, emotional, mental, and spiritual spheres, as well.

Genesis not only gives us a foundation for gender equality, but also teaches us to think in terms of design. You will not find gender roles or stereotypes laid out in the Creation account. Rather, we see that men and women have different designs inherent in their gender; that is, the way they generate new life. Within the language of gender design, there is plenty of room for the variety of personalities and vocations we possess, male or female. It does not describe what we are restricted from, but what we are designed for.

Chapter 4

The Image of God and Marriage

Male and female together

As we have seen in the previous chapter, Genesis 1:28 states that the image of God is contained in both males and females equally. At the same time, however, given the overall context of the creation account in Genesis 1 and 2, we can take this one step further to see the image of God as not simply enshrined in us as individuals, but especially in the union of male and female together in marriage.

To understand why this is the case, we need to look at the story of the creation of Eve in Genesis 2 and its implications elsewhere in Scripture.

> *Then the LORD God said, "It is not good that man should be alone; I will make a helper fit for him." ... So the LORD God caused a deep sleep to fall upon the man, and while he slept took one of his ribs and closed up its place*

with flesh. And the rib that the LORD God had taken from the man he made into a woman and brought her to the man. Then the man said, "This at last is bone of my bones and flesh of my flesh; she shall be called Woman, because she was taken out of Man." Therefore a man shall leave his father and his mother and hold fast to his wife, and they shall become one flesh." (Gen. 2:18, 21-24 ESV)

Commentators noticed early on the difference between this description of the creation of Eve and Genesis 1:28, which can be taken to mean that man and woman were created together. One unusual resolution suggested comes from the Midrash Rabbah, which states that man was originally created as a hermaphrodite and then God separated the sexes. While we certainly don't need to go quite *that* far for an explanation for the differences in the two chapters, there is an important element of truth here. In a very real sense, the "man" as created in the image of God includes male and female together as a unit.

A partnership in love

Let's take a closer look at Genesis 2. First, we should note that this is the only place in the creation accounts in which God pronounces something *not* good. It is not good for man to be alone, *because he was made to be a social being.* Animals were not adequate as his companions, so God created Eve from Adam's side (a better translation than "rib"). Eve was thus part of him and so could not be considered either inferior or a part of the creation over which Adam was to have dominion.

For all the misogyny that sometimes creeps into the writings of medieval theologians, many of the most important ones got it right on this point. To take just one example, Peter Lombard's *The Sentences*, which was the basic textbook for theology in the Middle Ages, cites Saint Augustine when he addressed the question of why God used one of Adam's ribs to make Eve:

> *Moreover from these causes "woman was made from man, not from any part of the man's body, but she was formed from his side, so that there might be shown, that she was created in a partnership of love, lest perchance, if she had been made from [his] head, she might seem to be preferred to man for [his] domination, or if from [his] feet, to be subjected [to him] for [his] service. Therefore because for man there was prepared neither a lady nor a handmade, but a companion, she was to be produced neither from [his] head nor from [his] feet, but from [his] side, so that she might recognize that she [was] to be placed alongside him, she whom he had learned to recognize as the one taken from his side."* [1]

---

[1] *Sentences*, book 2, distinction 18, question 2; see http://www.franciscan-archive.org/lombardus/opera/ls2-18.html, citing Augustine, *On the Literal Meaning of Genesis* 9.13.23. See also Thomas Aquinas, *Summa Theologica* 1, q. 92, 3, http://www.newadvent.org/summa/1092.htm#article3.

These comments, of course, reinforce the point that since the image of God is shared between men and women, they are intrinsically equal before God. But they also point ahead to Adam's reaction to the creation of Eve. In Genesis 2:23, Adam recognizes Eve as part of himself, and so names her *Woman* (Hebrew *ishshah*) because she was taken out of *Man* (Hebrew *ish*). Since in Hebrew thought, a being's name was supposed to reflect its nature, the derivation of the word for woman indicates the deep, intimate connection between woman and man.

Woman's origin from Man leads directly to the next verse: Man is to leave his parents and be joined to Woman—in other words, he is to marry and form a new family unit. And this is accomplished by the two "becoming one flesh" through sexual relations, in essence providing wholeness by reuniting Adam with his Rib.

So, the image of God in Genesis 1:28 is encompassed equally by men and women, but most fully by man and woman together, as a family. The family is the fundamental unit within society and is thus the place at which human dominion/stewardship over the world is first exercised.

Scripture on marriage

There are several points that follow from the nature of marriage in Scripture.

The first, as Jesus affirmed, is that marriage is meant to be permanent: God joins men and women together into one flesh, and so we should not try to undo what God has done (Mk. 10:2-9). Even from an anthropological perspective this makes sense. All cultures have marriage as a privileged institution, even though it might take a variety of forms, because it creates a stable environment to bring children into the world and to provide for them. Allowing marriages to dissolve easily disrupts its role in child-rearing. For Christians, our understanding of the unity of the two-in-one-flesh should make us do everything we can to ensure the permanence of marriage.

Second, the deep, intimate unity within marriage points to the depth of the Church's relationship and unity with Jesus. In the Old Testament, God often describes Israel as His wife, particularly by identifying Israel's idolatry with adultery (e.g., Hos. 1:2). In the New Testament, the Church is described as the body of Christ, and He is united with it in the same way that husbands and wives are one flesh (Eph. 6:31-32). The Apostle Paul characterized marital love as a mirror of unity and intimate fellowship that we experience in our relationship with Christ. Early on, these ideas led the Church to move away from the polygamy practiced in the pagan world (and to some extent in ancient Israel) and to insist on monogamy as the only proper form for marriage: one man, one woman, one lifetime.

The Church's teaching on the permanence of marriage and its emphasis on monogamy had an enormous effect on improving women's place in society. No longer could a woman be divorced because she had no sons or was past childbearing age. No longer could wealthy men take multiple wives, diminishing the "extra" women's status in the household and depriving poorer men of spouses. As Vishal Mangalwadi points out, monogamy led to social structures in the West that had a tremendously positive effect on society, so much so that in India even Hindus pushed to mandate monogamy as an essential prerequisite for modernization.[2] Given that this is God's design for humanity, it should come as no surprise that it produces better results than the alternatives.

Third, marriage reflects the Trinity. The doctrine of the Trinity says that the three persons of the Godhead are all one, yet in some sense distinct from each other. Just as a cube with a width of one meter, a height of one meter, and a depth of one meter, has a volume of one cubic meter, so the three persons of the Trinity complement each other, each participating in all the attributes of deity. Yet, the Godhead is only fully defined by the interrelationships of the three together as One. The significance of this is that God is an intrinsically relational being, in and of Himself, living in eternal loving relations between Father, Son and

---

[2] *Must the Sun Set on the West*, audio CD series, *From Luther's Vicarage to Hefner's Harem: Turning Men into (Play)boys and Women into Desperate Housewives.*

Spirit. Thus, humanity made in His image is, as we have seen, relational. And man and woman as the two equals becoming one flesh in marriage provides us with a two-dimensional picture of our three-dimensional God.

Foundation for sexual ethics

Lastly, Genesis 2:24 is the foundation for sexual ethics. Sexual activity is designed to unite a man and a woman together in a permanent bond. Even our biology points to this, as the hormonal response to sexual activity increases emotional attachment to your partner. This is one reason why sexual activity is restricted to marriage—the potential to cause devastating emotional damage to ourselves and each other is so great, it requires the protection of a permanent, committed, loving relationship. Our society's experience today with "sexual liberation" demonstrates the wisdom of the biblical view.

Although it is rarely seen in this light, marriage is the place where the full image of God found in male and female together is best seen and expressed. This is all the more reason for us to work to restore our commitment to and advocacy for a biblical vision of sexuality and marriage in our churches and society.

Questions

1. Why was it "not good" for the man to be alone in Genesis? Explain why this "not good" condition reflects the image of God.

2. There is a great deal of confusion about the nature of marriage today. How does society view the nature and purpose of marriage today? Read Matt. 19:3-9. What was Jesus' understanding of marriage? How does it compare to the views of our culture?

3. Sexual activity is a driving force in American culture and politics, as evidenced by media, regulatory policy concerning healthcare, court decisions, and political platforms. What do Jesus' words in the above passage suggest about our culture's unconstrained attitudes toward sex? Read 1 Cor. 6:12-20. What does this passage add to Jesus' teaching about sexual activity?

4. Read Eph. 5:21-33. Describe the responsibilities of husbands and wives in this passage. How does verse 21 affect the way you interpret the passage? How does this passage fit with the argument in the chapter that biblical marriage and monogamy are good for women?

5. What does Eph. 5:21-33 tell us about the work of Christ and his relationship to the church? What does Christ's work tell us about the nature of marriage?

6. What can Christians today do to help recover a biblical understanding of marriage in the church and in society?

EXTRA THOUGHTS
By Maria Baer, Senior Writer & Podcast Host

I first learned about atoms in fifth grade. My teacher called them the "building block of matter," and to demonstrate, pointed to the front of the classroom. She said if one atom of the blackboard were damaged, it would no longer be a blackboard. That sounded like magic to me. How does someone destroy an atom? What does a blackboard-that's-no-longer-a-blackboard look like? She might have missed something about the science, but that image has stuck with me.

Christians who embrace God's good design for marriage are rightly concerned with modern sexual heresies, including that the biological sex of those involved in a marriage does not matter. But that lie is not the first ruined atom. It is the leftover not-marriage-matter of an institution whose destruction requires a prior lie: that marriage's only "meaning" is to make us happy.

If we reduce marriage that far, we destroy the blackboard. We will turn marriage into anything and everything because when it comes to our own joy, we have a terrible habit of settling for far too less. And marriage as an exercise in mere selfish pleasure is a poor substitute for God's deliberate architecture of one man and one woman who come together to "re-become" a fuller picture of Himself.

Chapter 5

The Image of God and Spirituality

In God's image

In our previous chapters, we observed that the image of God means that we are created to be God's representatives, regents, and stewards on earth; that this position is the foundation for human dignity and rights; that it applies equally to men and women; and that it is expressed most directly in the family as the fundamental unit in society, and therefore the place where our dominion over creation is first exercised.

The tools God has given humanity to carry out this work of stewardship—creativity, reason, the ability to make choices, the will, emotions, morality—all of these share one important characteristic: they are all expressions of the non-physical side of human nature; that is, the fact that in addition to having physical bodies, we are spiritual beings as well.[1]

Challenges to spirituality

Contemporary culture poses several challenges to the biblical idea of spirituality. One common worldview known as *materialism* or *naturalism*, says that the physical world of matter and energy is all that exists, and thus people have no non-physical side. This view is commonly associated with the scientific community, particularly those who believe that the natural sciences provide the only reliable approach to knowledge about any and everything, an idea known as scientism.

To believe this runs counter to our experience of life. First, it argues that our consciousness is nothing more than brain chemistry; that free will is an illusion since everything we do is the result of physics and chemistry. Love, hate, self-consciousness and self-awareness, all of these are just chemical reactions. Good and evil and right and wrong do not exist since they are neither matter nor energy. You cannot even call them cultural preferences since a preference is neither matter nor energy.

---

[1] Scripture divides humans up in a variety of ways: body, soul and spirit; body and soul; heart, soul, mind and strength, etc. For our purposes here, we are not looking at a precise distinction between the different aspects of human nature, but simply using "spirit" to describe all of humanity's non-physical traits.

Even the thoughts you have as you read this aren't thoughts in the way you think—they're just neurons firing as a result of electrical impulses from your optic nerves. Your "freedom" even inside your own head is just an illusion. You can no more change your mind than the moon can stop orbiting the earth. You are nothing more than a robot carrying out the necessary and inevitable results of biology, chemistry, physics, and math. While some people claim that this is true, it is extremely doubtful that they really believe it deep down, and it is certain that they do not and cannot live as if it were true.

A second problem concerns the word "spiritual" itself. People frequently describe themselves as "spiritual but not religious" or talk about someone being "very spiritual." The problem is, if you ask what they mean by the word "spiritual" they typically cannot define it without falling back on "religious" concepts. It seems to mean an interest in metaphysical issues, habitually living in the moment, or a sense of connection to a non-physical "higher being" or "beings."

Even though a "spiritual" person's spiritual practices (i.e., practices to get in touch with the higher beings or to attain metaphysical experiences or knowledge) may be done as part of a group, spirituality is rarely seen in corporate terms. It tends to be highly individual, which serves to separate spirituality from religion. This emphasis on intuition and experience makes it close to the ancient heresy of

Gnosticism, a teaching that salvation is attained through acquiring secret knowledge or discovery from within.

While this idea of spirituality has some positive elements, particularly its recognition of the existence of the non-physical dimensions of reality, it rarely reflects the biblical concept of humans as spiritual creatures. It often leans toward a form of *dualism*, another element of ancient Gnosticism. Gnostics believed that the spiritual world was superior to the physical world, so much so that the physical is irrelevant at best or completely evil at worst. This idea shows up in Christian Science, in many Eastern religions and New Age teachings, and, ironically in some forms of Christian fundamentalism.

Yet Scripture tells us that God created the physical world and pronounced it very good—including our bodies. In fact, our bodies are essential for us to carry out our mandate to be God's stewards over the physical world. We must be *in* them to take care *of* it. How, then, can the body be evil?

Humanity's fall into sin doesn't change the essential goodness of the body. Sin comes from our inner, non-physical being, not our bodies (Mark 7:14-23).[2] We will return to the effects of the Fall in chapter 11.

---

[2] Paul's use of the term "flesh" as the opposite of "spirit" (e.g. Rom. 8:5) does not refer to the physical body. In context, it refers to an attitude of rebellion against the Holy Spirit's leading of our lives in obedience to God.

An integrated whole

Instead of dividing body and spirit, the Bible teaches that the human being is an integrated whole, simultaneously physical and spiritual, both created good. This unity is reflected in the word for "spirit" in both Hebrew (*ruah*) and Greek (*pneuma*), which refers not just to spirit, but to breath. While it is possible to take this too far, the connection of spirit and breath points to the fact that it is the union of spirit and body that gives us life (e.g. Gen. 2:7).

To put it differently, we cannot separate our understanding of what it means for us to be spiritual creatures from our bodies. Neither the *materialist* who ignores the reality of the spirit, nor the *Gnostic* who rejects the significance of the body, are correct. The spirit and the body are united in us, and these must be understood together.

Of course, even animals have "the breath of life" (Gen. 7:21-22). The human spirit goes well beyond simply giving us biological life. As medieval theologians and Renaissance thinkers pointed out, humanity is unique as a microcosm of the creation. We are both physical and spiritual creatures, we are both sensual and rational, we participate in both time and eternity. What creature is thus in a better position to act as God's regent (or, in ancient Near Eastern terms, His image) on earth?

Biblical spirituality

So, what is the biblical concept of spirituality? Jesus tells us that "God is spirit, and those who worship him must worship in spirit and in truth" (Jn. 4:24 ESV). Our ability to worship God, to connect with Him, even to have a personal relationship with Him, hinges on the fact that we have within us a spirit that is in some measure a reflection, an image, of God's Spirit. Without the ability of our spirit to connect with God as spirit, worship cannot happen.

This is the nature of true spirituality – worshiping God who is Spirit. Even this, however, cannot be separated from our bodies. Rom. 12:1 tells us that true worship occurs as we present our bodies as living sacrifices to God. The Greek word translated as "body" is *soma*, which points to the person as an integrated whole – bodies, minds, emotions, and will. This echoes Jesus' restatement of the *shema*, the foundation of Judaism, which tells us that we are to love God with all our heart, soul, mind and strength—the whole being (Mark 12:29).[3]

All we think, say, and do is thus to be done for the love of God, as part of presenting our whole selves as

---

[3] One implication of this is that taking proper care of our bodies is an aspect of true spirituality. While we do not worship the body, we must take care of it and develop it just as we do our minds and our "spiritual life" as part of our stewardship of ourselves before God.

living sacrifices to Him, which is true worship and true spirituality. This is another way of expressing our calling as God's stewards on earth: all that we do here, we are to do in His name, for His sake, to express our love for Him and to glorify Him.

Questions

1. Of the two extremes of materialism and Gnosticism, which have you run into the most? Describe some specific examples that you have encountered. Do you see either present in the church?

2. How would you define the words "spiritual" and "spirituality?" How do people grow spiritually?

3. Read John 4:1-26. What does Jesus identify as the critical requirements for true worship? Why do you think He lists these rather than anything else?

4. Read Mark 12:28-31. What can you do to grow in loving God with your heart? With your soul? With your mind? With your strength? What is the relationship between loving God and spirituality?

5. Read Rom. 12:1-2. What is the role of the body in our "spiritual service" (Greek: latreia, service or worship to God)? Have you ever considered the role of the body in worship? Does developing the body have a place in our spirituality? In loving God?

6. What is the danger we face in Rom. 12:2? Do you see this problem in the church today? How do we avoid this trap, and conversely, how are we transformed? Why do you think the mind (Greek nous, the part of the mind that understands what is true and real; intuition; imagination; common sense) is so important to Paul?

7. Do you see spirituality as a individual, corporate, or both? How do your spiritual life and activities reflect your answer?

EXTRA THOUGHTS
By S. Michael Craven, Director, Colson Fellows Program

Ever since Karl Marx penned his denunciatory statement on religion in 1843, opponents of religion have worked to convince us that religious faith is an outdated relic of the past whose inexplicable existence remains only by means of an unenlightened and uneducated lower class. Instead, spirituality is part of what it means to be human.

Indeed, there is abundant data supporting the claim that religious belief in America is in a state of free-fall. As early as 2009, the American Religious Identity Survey reported, "In one of the most dramatic shifts, 15 percent of Americans now say they have no religion—a figure that's almost doubled in 18 years." There is no doubt that Christianity, as it has come to be understood in America, has been in decline and that may not be a bad thing. Frankly, the decline of nominal, shallow Christianity may actually be good news.

In contrast to the idea that religion persists among the uneducated, University of Virginia sociologist W. Bradford Wilcox found that since the 1970s, it is the least educated who dominate the rapidly growing category of those having "no religious preference." Whereas among the most educated, religious faith remains relatively stable.

Perhaps the growing indifference to God and lack of interest in the larger questions fueled by willful ignorance and mindless amusement is the true opiate of the masses?

Chapter 6

The Image of God and Creativity

In God's image

Although the term "image of a god" in the ancient Near East conveyed the idea of being a representative or steward of a deity, the Biblical phrase also points to those things in human beings that make us similar to God and thus enable us to carry out our charge as His regents in the world. In this and the next several chapters, we will explore aspects of our nature that reflect God's own attributes and look at some of their implications for our work as God's stewards. We begin with creativity.

Creativity and human life

Christians do not talk much about creativity as a crucial aspect of humanity. Few formal theologians address it in connection with the image of God. Part of the reason for this is history. Originally, theologians argued that **only**

God could "create" (Latin *creare*), which for them meant producing something out of nothing (Latin e*x nihilo*). Humans could only "make" (Latin *facere*) things from existing material.

Yet as Dorothy Sayers pointed out, "It is observable that in the passage leading up to the statement … [that man is made in the image of God], he has given no detailed information about God. Looking at man, he sees in him something essentially divine, but when we turn back to see what he says about the original upon which the 'image' of God was modelled, we find only the single assertion, 'God created'. The characteristic common to God and man is apparently that: the desire and the ability to make things."[1]

Similarly, J.R.R. Tolkien, who travelled in the same circles as Sayers, emphasized the idea of "sub-creation" in producing his fantasy works, striving to create a coherent, consistent secondary world. He saw this process of sub-creation "as a form of worship, a way for creatures to express the divine image in them by becoming creators."[2]

---

[1] *The Mind of the Maker*, http://www.worldinvisible.com/library/dlsayers/mindofmaker/mind.02.htm. This book is the most thorough treatment of creativity as central to what it means to be human and to the image of God that I have seen. It is no accident that Sayers was a novelist, playwright, poet and translator—in other words, a person engaged in "creative writing"—rather than a formal theologian.

[2] David C. Downing, "Sub-Creation or Smuggled Theology: Tolkien contra Lewis on Christian Fantasy,"http://www.cslewisinstitute.org/cslewis/downing_theology.htm. This idea is also reflected in the story, "Of Aulë and Yavanna," chapter 2 of *The Silmarillion*.

So, what exactly is creativity? The term is curiously difficult to define, though obviously it has something to do with the ability to create—the "desire and the ability to make things," as Sayers put it. Not surprisingly, the early chapters of Genesis and the mandate to "have dominion" over the world emphasize the big-picture elements of creativity.

In the beginning

God gave Adam two jobs in Eden. First, Adam was "to work and keep" the Garden (Gen. 2:15). The Garden is specifically described not just as a place where food grew, but as a place of beauty and delight (Gen. 2:9). We may thus infer that working and keeping the Garden involved not simply food production but cultivating beauty as well. In other words, the arts have been part of God's mandate to humanity from the very beginning.

There can be no question that God loves beauty. Consider the Earth and stars as celebrated in the Psalms, or the specifications of the Tabernacle and its furnishings, as well as the priests' garments (Ex. 26-28, 30), or the Temple in 1 Kg. 6-7, or the throne room of Heaven in Is. 6 and Rev. 4, or the New Jerusalem in Rev. 21. God's works and His worship are bathed in beauty.

God told Moses, "See, I have called by name Bezalel the son of Uri, son of Hur, of the tribe of Judah, and I have ***filled him with the Spirit of God***, with ability and intelligence, with knowledge and all craftsmanship, to devise artistic designs, to work in gold, silver and bronze, in cutting stones for setting and in carving wood, to work in every craft. And I have appointed with him Oholiab, the son of Ahisamach, of the tribe of Dan. And I have given to all able men ability, that they may make all I have commanded you...." (Ex. 31:2-6, emphasis added). The craftsmanship and skill that went into making the Tabernacle, as well as the ability "to devise artistic designs," were the products of being filled with the Holy Spirit, and therefore reflect something of God's own nature.

The artist uses materials and skills has given and is thus a sub-creator (to use Tolkien's word), exercising the image of God by fulfilling the mandate to work and keep the Garden.

Adam's second task was naming the animals (Gen. 2:19-20). This was a creative act, though of a different type. In Hebrew, a being's name was thought to reflect its nature. Thus to name the animals appropriately required studying and understanding them, then using the right word to encapsulate their nature.

While we will return to this in chapter 9's discussion of the sciences, for now we should note that naming is an intellectual and creative activity and a full biblical understanding of human creativity includes not just the visual arts but the verbal arts as well.[3]

Language is a characteristic of God Himself. He spoke the universe into existence, and Jesus is described in John 1 as the word of God. Human use of language is a reflection of the image of God, particularly when we use words to create.

Creativity in language

The nature of Scripture affirms the importance of creativity in language. God did not reveal Himself through a list of essential doctrines or a schematic outline of theology. Instead, He chose to reveal Himself through many authors over hundreds of years in about every type of literature then known to humanity. There are historical narratives, laws, poems and songs, proverbs, prophetic oracles, parables, letters, apocalyptic literature, even genealogies. In producing our own literature, we are following the example of God who gave us a rich literary heritage in His word.

This is precisely the creativity both Dorothy Sayers and J.R.R. Tolkien had in mind when they talked about "making things" or "sub-creation," though they would not have limited creative activity to literature. However, both saw writing as a highly creative act because it involves bringing imagination to life using words as God Himself did at the creation.

---

[3] There is common ground between visual and verbal arts. Bezalel had intelligence and knowledge, which empowered his craftsmanship; Adam needed the same qualities in naming animals, though he applied them using a different vehicle than the physical objects Bezalel produced. It thus seems fair to say that some type of intellectual ability is a prerequisite for creative work.

Creativity in music

Another area of creative activity in Scripture is music. God is surrounded by music in Heaven (Is. 6; Rev. 4, 5, 11, 15.). God's actions in history were celebrated in song (e.g., Ex. 15:1-21), and music was central to the worship in Jerusalem (e.g., 1 Chron. 15:16-24). Jesus and the apostles sang hymns (Matt. 26:30), as did Paul and Silas, even when they were locked in the deepest part of a Roman prison (Acts 16:25).

Psalms, the longest book in the Bible, is a collection of songs, and celebrates not only singing but instrumental music (e.g., Ps. 150) to praise God. The Psalms include songs of praise, laments, pleas for help, introspection, prayers of repentance and more. In any circumstance it gives us examples of how to sing our heart's cries to God.

The Apostle Paul even tells us that music is a sign of being filled with the Spirit (Eph. 5:18-20). Singing joins Bezalel's visual arts as a work of the Holy Spirit and therefore as an aspect of the image of God.

Creativity in all of life

Creativity extends well beyond these few examples. In every area of life creativity plays a major role. The reason is simple: part of our nature as image bearers of God the Creator is to be sub-creators, and to carry out our original mandate which God gave us in the Garden, to create culture as a function of our stewardship of the world.

Questions

1. How would you define creativity? Would you agree with Tolkien that creative activity is a form of worship? Why or why not?

2. Describe the jobs that God gave to Adam in the Garden. Why is creativity essential to carrying them out?

3. Read Ex. 31:2-6. Describe the results of being filled with the Spirit in Bezalel's life. What does this suggest about the nature of spiritual gifts? Have you ever considered the possibility that you are specifically gifted by God to carry out your job?

4. Historically, the church has been a major patron of both visual and musical arts, and Christianity has been an inspiration for great literature and drama. Was this an appropriate use of resources? Why or why not? Do you think that the church and individual Christians are sufficiently involved in sponsoring great art today?

5. Read Ps. 150. List the ways we are told to praise God. How many of these do you incorporate into your personal life? How many are used in your church? Do you think we should use more of these today? Why or why not?

6. In addition to the arts, what other fields require creativity? In what ways do those fields reflect the image of God as discussed in the first chapters of this book?

EXTRA THOUGHTS
By Timothy D. Padgett

Very often, when we think of the image of God, creativity is one of the first things to come to mind. For many observers, the arts allow God's nature to shine through His human agents like little else, and it is not hard to see why. Who has not been taken up in a moment of beauty, whether it was a piece of music or stunning painting, a remarkable film or the simple stillness of a careful garden? There is something about the creative arts which seems almost divine.

As humans, we do not just walk but we dance. We do not merely speak but we sing. We do not merely eat but we dine. This is a most wonderful inheritance of God's imprint on the human soul, and one which, all too often, has been sadly neglected among Christians.

Yet, we ought not make the opposite error. Some, in reaction to a diminished view of the arts, see creativity only in the hands of the artist and not the craftsman. The machinist, the engineer, the builder–each of these expresses the image of God as much as the poet or the sculptor. Remember, so much of God's creative acts which we rightly enjoy involved building, constructing, and designing the wonderfully functional world in which we live.

Chapter 7

The Image of God and Reason

God and reason

Of all the creatures in the physical world, only human beings share with God the **ability to reason**. It is not surprising, then, that when theologians discuss aspects of the image of God, reason almost always tops the list. As God's stewards of the world, we have been given reason—one of the most important tools we have. As we explore the implications of our creation in God's image, we must take a closer look at human rationality. But before we do that, we must look at reason as an attribute of God.

Time and again Scripture records that **God is rational**, first in God's work of creation. In Genesis, God looked at what He has made and evaluated it as "good" (Gen. 1:10, 12), "not good" (Gen. 2:18), or "very good" (Gen. 1:31). This evaluation necessarily involved a rational judgment about the creation. The Scriptures frequently extol God's wisdom, the practical application of divine knowledge. Proverbs tells us that God created the world through wisdom (Prov. 3:19-20), and the Psalms celebrate God's wisdom displayed in creation (Ps. 104:24).

The supreme example in Scripture of God's rationality is in John 1:1-3: "In the beginning was the Word (Greek: logos), and the Word was with God and the Word was God. He was in the beginning with God. All things were made through Him, and without him was not anything made that was made."

Logos, the Greek word translated here as "Word," is a far richer term than "word" is in English. In Platonic thought, the logos was the **creative principle** through which the world came into existence. In Stoicism, it was the **rational principle** which governed the universe. In common use, it is the root word for "logic," and pointed to both **knowledge and thought**.

Christ as the *Logos* of God is the sum total of all that can be known (Col. 2:3), the ultimate example of divine reason and wisdom (1 Cor. 1:24).

Reasoning with us

Not surprisingly, then, God sometimes **appeals to reason** to try to get through to us. For example, in Is. 44:9-20, God criticizes idolatry, appealing to common sense to show how foolish it is. In Is. 1:18-20, He invites Judah to reason with Him—repentance and obedience produces forgiveness and blessing; rebellion brings destruction. Which course makes more sense?

God's rationality is **far beyond our own**. In Is. 55:8-9, God tells us, "… my thoughts are not your thoughts, neither are your ways my ways, declares the LORD. For as the heavens are higher than the earth, so are my ways higher than your ways and my thoughts than your thoughts." Human **reason can only take us so far** when it comes to knowing and understanding God and why He governs the world as He does. For that, we need **revelation**, which comes to us both through the natural world and Scripture. This is why Prov. 3:5 exhorts us to "Trust in the LORD with all your heart and do not lean on your own understanding." **Reason has is limits**, especially when it comes to understanding God and His ways.

What is reason?

God is rational—super-rational, but rational, nonetheless. What does God's rationality tell us about human reason? And, what exactly is reason?

As is frequently the case with terms like this, reason is **not easy to define** simply. On a human level, reason is the ability to reach **conclusions** based on **premises**. The premises can be abstract ideas as in mathematics, or they can be based on personal experience and observation, such as "if you put your hand in a fire, you will get burned," or some combination of the two as is frequently the case in the sciences.[1]

Reason is a deceptively **powerful tool** that we use constantly in exercising our mandate as stewards of the world. Reason enables us to do everything from understanding cause and effect, to learning that planting seeds leads to growing plants, to understanding the importance of water in the natural world, to figuring out irrigation systems, to learning what works and what doesn't in putting up buildings, to developing mathematics and applying it to real world situations.

The same ability that led our ancestors to fashion stone tools enabled us to develop iPads and space probes. It all come from reason based on **observation, experience**, and sometimes **abstract premises**.

The importance of reason

Reason is thus **critically important** to our work with

---

[1] Scientific theories are supposed to be supported by observations though in practice particularly powerful theories become paradigms through which all subsequent observations and evidence are interpreted. At that point, the governing theory becomes a form of abstract premise. The reigning paradigms in science are considered foundational and for all practical purposes certain, until enough counterevidence develops, leading to the emergence of a new theory which overturns the old paradigm.

the physical world: without it, we cannot exercise our proper dominion under God. But reason extends beyond just understanding the laws of nature. For example, we can engage in **moral reasoning**, thinking through the ethical implications of actions, ideas and policies based on principles of right and wrong. We can use reason to try to **understand the people** around us—what motivates them, why they do or say the things they do, etc. And through both principles and experience, we can learn how to **interact effectively** with others.

Reason is an effective tool because it deals with our experiences as physical creatures. We interact with the natural world and with other people . We can study, experiment, observe, and think through our experiences. This is true of ethical issues, since they too deal with life in this world. Things get more complex, however, when it comes to **spiritual matters**.

Many philosophers argue that spirituality is a matter of faith, and faith is divorced from reason. They reject any connection between reason and "authority," mystical experience, intuition, or faith. There is an element of truth in this. If you follow a New Age teacher's techniques and enter an altered state of consciousness, it does not logically follow that the teacher's explanation of that experience is automatically correct. Neither the authority of the teacher nor the experience itself provides enough to evaluate what happened rationally.

However, the argument against authority and faith is clearly overdrawn. For example, in practice those who make this argument against authority frequently rely on authority. How many can prove that the Earth goes around the Sun, as opposed to accepting it as true because of the authority of scientists? If they can prove it, do they rely on their own observations, or do they accept another's authority? Or how many rely on experts (authorities) for medical care, or any other areas of life where we look to experts' explanations?

Beyond this inconsistency lies the problem that all reason is ultimately based on **unproven assumptions** that must be taken on **faith**. We cannot prove that our observations are accurate, that our minds are capable of understanding the world, that cause and effect are really linked, that other minds exist. All knowledge is ultimately **based on faith**—on accepting unproven and unprovable assumptions as true. To argue that faith and reason are separate, incompatible spheres is simply false. **Reason relies on faith** as its starting point.

As a result, despite the fact that God is infinite and we are not, we can even reason about Him. In fact, Christianity demands the development of theology, which Rodney Stark defines as "formal reasoning about God."[2] As Stark points out, "...unlike Muhammad or Moses, whose texts

---

[2] *The Victory of Reason*, 5.

were accepted as divine transmissions and therefore have encouraged literalism, Jesus wrote nothing, and from the very start the Church Fathers were forced to reason as to the implications of a collection of his remembered sayings—the New Testament is not a unified scripture but an *anthology*. Consequently, the precedent for deduction and inference and for the idea of theological progress began with Paul: 'For our knowledge is imperfect and our prophecy is imperfect.'"[3]

Christianity **requires the use of human reason** to draw a coherent picture of God and His dealings with humanity from the biblical texts. This study of the texts leads to greater and greater insight into the Bible as each generation builds on the work of previous scholars. And, according to Stark, this idea of theological progress led to a more general idea of intellectual progress, ultimately resulting in the use of reason in science, economics, and politics, creating much of the modern Western world.[4]

Far from being in opposition, reason and faith are **deeply intertwined**. Both are necessary and important tools that God has given us to understand the world, each other, and Him, and to fulfill our purpose as His stewards in the world.

---

[3] Ibid., 9.
[4] Ibid., 12.

Questions

1. Read Prov. 3:19-20 and Ps. 104, noting particularly verse 24. How is God's wisdom displayed in the creation? When you look at the world, do you see evidence of a rational mind behind it, or simply time and random chance?

2. Read John 1:1-3; 1 Cor. 1:20-25; Col. 2:1-4. What do these verses tell us about Jesus and His relationship with God's rationality? How does this expand your understanding of who Jesus is?

3. What role does reason play in our relationships with other people? Is it more authentic to act on the basis of our emotions than reason as we deal with people? Why or why not? Similarly, how does reason play in ethical and moral decision-making?

4. The chapter argues that faith and reason are intertwined—that you cannot have reason without faith, and that faith is supported by reason. Do you agree or disagree? Why?

5. Read Eph. 1:17-19, 3:16-19; Phil. 1:9-11; Col. 1:9-12. Notice how often Paul uses words like knowledge, wisdom, discernment, and understanding. Why do you think Paul puts so much emphasis on this in his prayers for these churches?

6. What is the role of reason in our spiritual life? Is it a help or a hindrance? What is the right balance between theology, mystery, and practice?

EXTRA THOUGHTS
By William E. Brown, Senior Fellow for Worldview and Culture

Two thoughts about reason. First, reasoning is worldview-dependent. People's worldview commitment determines the environment of their reasoning. A logical argument may be compelling from an atheistic worldview but completely unreasonable from a Christian worldview. For example, the website for Richard Dawkins's "Foundation for Reason and Science" is filled with atheistic assumption – there is no God, morality is a human derivation, and death is the predetermined extinction for every person. Dawkins considers faith to be evidence of "mental illness." Reading his arguments from a Christian worldview, they appear illogical, ill-informed, and misleading.

Second, reason does not work alone. The Apostle Paul gave priority status not to finely tuned syllogisms and human philosophy but to God's Spirit and power. Mathematician and philosopher Blaise Pascal concluded, "The heart has its reasons which reason knows nothing of... We know the truth not only by reason, but by the heart." The great commandment is to love the Lord with all our heart, soul, and mind (Matthew 22:37). The heart is where reason and emotions collaborate to direct the will to believe and act in faith.

Chapter 8

The Image of God and Work

In the last two chapters, we looked at creativity and reason, two essential tools that we, made in the image of God, are to use in creating culture as His stewards in the world. Before considering other aspects of human nature that reflect God's image, this chapter and the next will look at way creativity and reason work together to fulfill the work God gave us in Eden. We begin with a closer look at God's command to tend the Garden.

Our culture often sees work as something we do only because we have to. The biblical attitude toward work is that we do it because of who we are. Work is the fulfillment of our nature as beings made in God's image. Gen. 2:2 tells us that God worked when He created the world, or His Sabbath rest would be meaningless. His command to Adam to tend the Garden reflects His own nature as one who works.

Consider the fourth commandment. As Del Tackett points out in *The Truth Project*, we think of this as the Sabbath commandment, but we might think of it as the labor commandment: "Six days you shall labor, and do all your work, but the seventh day is a Sabbath to the LORD your God. On it you shall do no work ... For in six days the LORD made heaven and earth, the sea, and all that is in them, and rested on the seventh day. Therefore the LORD blessed the Sabbath day and made it holy" (Ex. 20:9-11). We take the Sabbath off because God did, but we also work the other six days because God did. And work is so important that God actually *had* to tell us to take time off!

There is another important aspect in which our work relates to God's: Adam's responsibility to tend the Garden was actually a command to continue and complete the work that God had begun. Our labor, using the resources He has placed in our hands, is an act of sub-creation intended to bring out the potential He created for the world.

This is evident all through biblical history. Creation begins formless and void and God puts it in order. When He puts Adam in the Garden, He doesn't intend for Adam to simply stay there. It is no accident that the Bible begins in a garden but ends in a city. God's ultimate goal is not to return us to some sort of pristine state of nature. Rather, we are to develop culture (a word which comes from the Latin *cultus*, meaning labor or cultivation), and ultimately to build civilization, which comes from the Latin *civitas*, meaning city.

The command to care for and tend the Garden does not mean merely to conserve what is there, but to develop it responsibly as stewards of God's world toward the advancement of civilization and culture. Jesus articulates this in the parable of the talents (Matt. 25:14-30). The punished servant is the one who simply conserved what he was given and did not try to bring profit to the master. Why should our stewardship of the world be any different?

Our work to develop culture and civilization is a sacred act to a Christian, to be carried out as part of our mandate as the image of God in this world. All professions that are not inherently sinful can be God-given vocations, callings on our life, to carry out God's purposes in and for the world. We need to escape from the idea that some jobs are sacred and others merely secular. All work is sacred to the Christian, done in full recognition that what we do matters and can be done for the glory of God. This idea, the cultural mandate, is critical in understanding our role as God's stewards, and for fulfilling Jesus' call to be salt and light in the world (Matt. 5:13-16, cf. Matt. 13:33).

The goodness and dignity of work also means we should apply our reason to the task, so that as good stewards we make the best and most efficient use of the resources available to us. We must always remember that the Earth is the Lord's, not ours, and though we should develop its resources, we should do it with care. Our reason and ingenuity must be used to responsibly create culture and make the best long-term use of what we have been given. Our work is important for advancing God's purposes in the world and is an essential part of what it means to be human. It also has economic significance. Genesis tells us that the Garden was both a source of food and a place of visual delight (Gen. 2:9). Adam was told to take care of the Garden and to eat the fruit that grew on the trees (Gen. 2:15-16). This is the very beginning of economics. As we tend the Garden, whether for the cultivation of beauty or the production of food, we are to earn our livelihood from our work.

The connection between the call to work and the provision of food points to a basic God-given right, the right to enjoy the fruits of our labor. This concept is known mainly in the popular paradigm of giving an honest day's pay for an honest day's work. It has also been used to support the idea of workers' ownership of the means of production, collectivization, and Christian-influenced versions of communism. These and related ideas, however, do not do justice to the full biblical vision of labor, ownership, and rewards.

The right to the fruits of our labor proceed from a right to property—in fact, it is hard to have the former without the latter. The Old Testament law presupposes a right to property. Otherwise, the commandment against theft and the many other property laws in the Torah would make no sense at all.

Consider the provisions for land ownership in Israel. A family's allotment of land was sacrosanct, so much so that when hard times hit, it could only be leased out, never sold. The destitute in Israel would never be without hope of a fresh start for the family because their land could never be taken away from them.. The right to property was absolute. Property rights extended to heirs, to ensure family inheritance.

How seriously God took this law can be seen in the life of Ahab, the most immoral king in Israel's history. He sponsored Baal worship and idolatry and persecuted the faithful, even murdering prophets (1 Kings 18:4). He was roundly condemned by Elijah and other prophets throughout his reign.

The most severe judgment came after his wife arranged for Naboth to be framed for blasphemy and executed so that Ahab could claim his vineyard (1 Kings 21:1-26).[1] God had already pronounced a death sentence against Ahab for disobeying his commands (1 Kings 20:42), but the judgment for the crimes against Naboth and his property led to an even more severe and horrifying judgment against Ahab and everyone in his household. Ahab had taken not only Naboth's life, but his family's place in Israel, so Ahab's family would itself be completely cut off from Israel.

---

[1] Since Ahab was not directly responsible for Naboth's death and humbled himself before God, God held off the judgment until the days of his son (1 Kings 21:27-28).

Significantly, it wasn't simply Naboth's murder that led to this judgment on Ahab's line. He was already guilty of multiple murders. What set this apart was the crime against Naboth's property rights in Israel.

Discussion of the right to property continues into the New Testament. Consistent testimony of the Scriptures points to this: from commands against theft to the example of Peter's continued ownership of his fishing boat (Jn. 21:3), or the wealthy Christians who opened their homes to the church. The one potential counterexample is Acts 2:44, which says that the believers in Jerusalem "had all things in common."

Many argue that the church operated as a community of goods without any private property, but a careful reading of the text shows that this was not the case. The verse following explains how "having all things in common" was worked out in practice. People sold their possessions (not "all" their possessions, or they themselves would become destitute) to provide for those in need. In other words, they maintained ownership of their property until there was a need.

The church continued to recognize property ownership, evident in Peter's statements to Ananias in Acts 5:4, which treats the idea that Ananias had full rights to his property as obvious and beyond question. So, even in a church that "had all things in common," property rights were inviolable. People owned their property but held it lightly so as to part with it freely to meet the needs of the poor. Thus, they simultaneously "had all things in common" and maintained private property.

Jews and Christians in the ancient world were unique in their perspective on the goodness and dignity of work, which other cultures saw only as drudgery fit for slaves and inferiors. At the same time, the recognition of property as an unalienable right, a right that preceded human government and thus as something that no king or government could arbitrarily revoke, created a stable environment for economic growth. We owe the positive vision of work, the incentives to be productive, and the security from arbitrary confiscation of our property—the hallmarks of traditional Western ideas of economics—to the long-term impact of the biblical worldview on society.

Questions

1. What is your attitude toward work? Is it a necessary evil or something more? By some studies 95% of younger workers are regularly looking to change jobs. What does that suggest about the state of work in America today?

2. Read Ecclesiastes 2:4-11, 18-23; Luke 12:16-22. When does work become a danger to us? Have you ever met someone who was "married" to their job, for whom everything and everyone, including family, was a distant second to career? If, as this chapter argues, work is what we were created for, how do you maintain a

The Image of God and Work

proper balance between your work life, your family, and other obligations?

3. Read Proverbs 6:6-11; 12:27; 13:4; 20:4; 21:25-26; 22:13; 24:30-34; 26:13-16; Matthew 25:24-30; Ephesians 4:28; 1 Thessalonians 4:10-12; 2 Thessalonians 3:6-12; 1 Timothy 5:8, 13. What do these verses tell us about how we should work? Is that how you work in your current calling?

4. Have you ever considered the idea that God worked in creating the world? What do you think of the idea that God deliberately left the creation incomplete for us to bring it to its final state in the City of God? How does that idea affect the way you view your work and your activities?

5. What is the connection between work and property rights? Medieval theologians argued that the right to property predated government and thus could not be violated by government (except for taxation to pay for its legitimate functions). Do you agree that property rights are unalienable? Does anyone have a right to the fruit of other people's work? Why or why not?

6. What is the relationship between work and the themes discussed in previous chapters such as stewardship, creativity, and reason?

EXTRA THOUGHTS
By Shane Morris, Senior Writer and Podcast Host

The Westminster Shorter Catechism declares that, "man's chief end is to glorify God, and to enjoy Him forever." Put another way, the main reason

God created human beings was so that we could worship Him and delight in doing so. This goes far beyond singing on Sunday morning. It means that everything we think, say, and do should be an act of praise to God—and that includes our work.

We too often act as if our lives were divided into distinct halves: the "secular" and the "sacred." Our modern culture encourages us to think this way, pressuring us to keep our religion within the walls of our church once a week, while the time we spend at work, at home, and at play belongs to us. We do not say it out loud, but we sometimes live as if God does not care about what we do in our "secular" lives, as long as we do not sin.

Nothing could be further from the truth. While corporate worship where we receive God's word and sacraments is special, He is equally present throughout our week. Everything we do is "coram Deo"—before God. That means work done well, diligent study, and even wholehearted recreation enjoyed to the Lord's praise is sacred and pleasing to Him. Work is worship because our whole lives are worship!

Chapter 9

The Image of God and Science

In previous chapters, we've referred to the image of God as humanity's call to be God's regents and representatives on Earth—to be His stewards. To equip us to carry out this task, God built a number of unique abilities into humanity, including creativity and reason. We use these in our physical labor to "tend and take care of the garden" (Gen. 2:15); these same abilities come into play as we engage in intellectual work, as Adam did when he named the animals (Gen. 2:19-20).

The task of naming the animals is much more involved than it sounds. In Hebrew, a being's name is supposed to reflect its nature. To give the animals their proper names, Adam needed to study them to understand their natures. Understanding the natural world is a vital part of our mandate to govern it as God's stewards. Not surprisingly, there are other observations of nature in Scripture. Many psalms talk about the natural world and relate it back to divine wisdom and God as creator and sustainer of all things (Ps. 104); other psalms and passages tell us that the creation speaks to us and teaches us about God (Ps. 19, Rom. 1:18-23). Many of Jesus' parables are drawn from nature as well. Wisdom—the practical application of divine knowledge—includes knowledge of the natural world. Solomon's wisdom included not only proverbs and judgments, but understanding trees and plants, mammals, birds, reptiles, and fish (1 Kings 4:33).

To that point, just as the mandate to tend the garden implies economic and artistic production and the creation of culture, so the mandate to name the animals is one for us to engage science.

It is common today for people to treat science and religion as if they were two separate, unconnected spheres. Science, it is argued, deals in facts; religion deals with "spiritual" things: morality and areas of faith, not knowledge. This is a false dichotomy. Science may focus on the physical world, but it is based on assumptions about the nature of the world and the nature of humanity that are anything but provable by scientific means. Any apparent conflict between science and religion proceeds from how those assumptions are set up.

For a Christian, the critical assumptions that enable us to do science are simple. God is rational, and so the world He created is rational. Human beings are made in God's image and thus we are also rational. Even if we cannot understand exhaustively everything God did, we can to some extent "think God's thoughts after Him" and discover the rational processes ("laws") that govern the physical universe.

This line of reasoning may seem obvious, but it is because our thinking has been firmly shaped by the Christian worldview. The reason modern science developed in the West is because Christianity provided the necessary it with the intellectual framework.. Medieval theologians working in what was then known as natural philosophy or natural theology laid a foundation for the scientific revolution, which was led by men such as Copernicus, Kepler, Galileo, Pascal, and Newton, all of whom were serious Christians firmly grounded in biblical ideas about God and the creation.

Contrast this with other cultures. In many Asian systems of thought, the world is a kind of illusion or dream in the mind of God. In Islam, Allah has direct control of everything that happens, and in medieval Islam the idea of natural law was considered apostasy because such laws would limit Allah's freedom. In pagan and animistic cultures, the world is largely sentient and as predictable as human behavior. None of these provides a solid foundation for the development of science (empirically-backed explanations of the workings of the physical world).

Then there is secularism, particularly scientism—the idea that the natural sciences provide the only reliable route to knowledge. Scientism posits that the universe somehow came into existence, then by the laws of physics galaxies, stars, and solar systems formed. On at least one planet, organic compounds came into existence by the same laws of physics, and then somehow these organic compounds spontaneously generated life (a process which never happens again). Finally, by random mutations this earliest form of life turned into human beings with brains capable of understanding the universe.

Yet under these circumstances it requires a leap of faith to believe that the universe is understandable or that our minds can in fact make sense of it. If our brains are the product of random mutation and chemical reactions, why should we assume they could comprehend anything reliably?[1]

As Alvin Plantinga points out, the most that undirected evolution would do is to give us minds that are geared for survival, not necessarily for discovering truth. While we might think that true ideas enhance survivability, this is not necessarily so. People may behave in a way that helps them survive even if the reasoning that leads to the behavior is false.

---

[1] http://www.breakpoint.org/features-columns/articles/999-is-christianity-the-enemy-of-science

Plantinga's example is a man named Paul, who, upon encountering a tiger runs away. He may do this because he does not want to be eaten, but there are other possible reasons as well. He may want to be eaten but doesn't think this particular tiger will do it. Or, he may think the tiger is a big pussycat and want to pet it, but thinks the best way to get the cat to let him is to run from it; or he might think he is in a race, and the tiger's appearance is the signal for him to start.

It doesn't matter what he believes or why, just so long as he runs. In other words, his survival does not prove the truth of his belief system. And this means that if both evolution and naturalism (that is, the idea that the natural world of matter and energy are all that exists) are true, we cannot rely on our minds to come to true conclusions, thus rendering all of science irrational.[2]

So, even though a purely secular worldview based on naturalism might *seem* to be the basis for engaging science, on closer examination it isn't. Scientism is a logically self-defeating position. It only seems plausible because it is living off the borrowed capital of the biblical worldview: that rational human beings can make sense of the rational universe – because both were made by a rational God.

---

[2] See http://www.hisdefense.org/OnlineLectures/tabid/136/ItemId/523/Default.aspx for Plantinga's audio lecture "Evolutionary Arguments against Naturalism" and his *Warrant and Proper Function* (New York: Oxford University Press, 1993).

The biblical teachings about God, the physical world, and human nature provide the firmest foundation for science of any competing worldview. But even more so, in the command to name the animals, God implicitly commands us to study and to come to understand the natural world as part of the work He has given us. This makes science an essential element of our stewardship of the world. It shows us something of God's amazing understanding, wisdom, and power. It helps us understand Him and his ways better and enables us to develop the resources He has given us, in the best ways we can to the glory of God.

Questions

1. What do you think is the relationship between science and religion? Can they work together? If so, how?

2. Our culture often claims directly or indirectly that science and religion are in conflict, and when there is a conflict, religion must give way to science. Can you think of any examples of this? What is your response to them?

3. What are some of the core ideas within Christianity that make it possible to engage science? Why is engaging science important for the Christian?

4. This chapter argues that taken on its own terms, "scientism" and the belief that matter and energy are all that exist effectively makes it impossible to be consistent and to approach science. Explain the argument. Do you agree or disagree? Why?

5. Read Ps. 9. In the Middle Ages, theologians often talked about two books written by God, the book of nature and the book of Scripture. Both required study to understand them properly, and each helped illuminate the other. What does the "speech" you hear from the heavens tell you?

6. Read Ps. 104 and Rom. 1:18-32. What are some of the lessons we should learn from the creation?

EXTRA THOUGHTS
By Shane Morris, Senior Writer and Podcast Host

For centuries, theologians have included the human ability to reason in what it means to be created "in the image of God." Science depends on this capacity for reason: we must make empirical observations, then form and test hypotheses in order to conduct scientific research. But, this makes reason one of the strongest arguments for rejecting atheistic naturalism, the claim that the material world is all that exists.

As C. S. Lewis points out in his book "Miracles," if our thoughts are part of the closed system of cause and effect we call the material world, then they are no more likely than a vomit or a sneeze to reflect truth. Only by assuming that our reason has its source beyond the collisions of atoms inside our brains can we trust its conclusions about the world.

Far from disproving the existence of immaterial or "supernatural" realities, science presupposes them at every turn. One immaterial reality it takes for granted is the reliability of the human mind, and the fact that it is distinct from (but related to) the organ.

Chapter 10
The Image of God and Freedom

The ability to make choices is of the most important aspects of our being made in the image of God is. Without this, creativity disappears, reason is reduced to mathematical calculations, work becomes robotic, and our role as God's regents in the world is reduced to being an automaton. Freedom—the ability to make choices—is thus an essential element of what it means to be human.

Our culture has an inconsistent relationship with freedom. Despite our obsession with absolute autonomy, the libertine insistence to decide for ourselves all matters of truth and even biology, the secular philosophical underpinnings of society do not allow a place for true freedom. Free will is under attack today from thinkers who reject the idea that humanity has a non-physical side, a "ghost in the machine."

Naturalism (also called materialism) – the premise that the physical world of matter and energy is all that exists – has no room for anything beyond our physical bodies that can make "free" choices, and thus naturalists routinely deny free will. At the same time they also insist that we can know right and wrong and thus are morally responsible, that we are "causal agents" and not bound by rigid determinism.[1]

Yet, what is the "we" that makes us causal agents? To a naturalist, the "we" is simply a consequence of chemical processes in the brain, processes which are themselves the product of other chemical processes, and ultimately of physical laws. In this way of thinking, matter and energy are all that exists, and human behavior is then governed solely by the laws of science, which can never be violated. Thus, everything about us, including our brain chemistry, is unchangeable since it is governed by the inviolable laws of science.

A consistent naturalist must argue we are nothing more than products of physical laws, that consciousness, free will, "causal agency," and moral responsibility are nothing more than illusions, epiphenomena of chemical processes which determine our thoughts but over which we have no control and can set no direction other than what has been predetermined by the laws of biochemistry.

Ultimately, this is a dead-end road, because it means we cannot even rely on our minds to make rational decisions,

---

[1] See, for example, http://www.naturalism.org/roundup.htm#2010.

since our reason itself is nothing more than electrochemical reactions produced by our brain chemistry. We may claim to make free choices in such a naturalist's world, but in the end it could only be a delusion.

In contrast, the Bible teaches that our thoughts, our desires, our values, and our choices all have significance, and that we have a genuine freedom to make decisions and to act accordingly. It is this freedom that allowed Adam to decide how to tend the Garden and develop culture, to choose names for the animals, and ultimately to make the moral choice about whether or not to follow God's instructions with respect to the Tree of the Knowledge of Good and Evil.

But how does free will work? If naturalists are wrong in thinking the mind is only a matter of brain chemistry, then what is free will? How does it then fit into the biblical picture of humanity? Particularly as it relates to our post-Fall natures, Christians have been discussing and debating such questions for millennia, so it is unlikely that we will come to any final answer here.

Perhaps the easiest entry point to understanding free will is through a variation on what medieval theologians called "faculty psychology." This view held that the mind, broadly understood, was separate from the body and consisted of a number of distinct "faculties" that were independent of but interacted with each other. The original list was long –

intelligence, perception, memory, will, etc. In the eighteenth and nineteenth centuries, the number was reduced to three: emotions, will, and intellect, roughly corresponding to the biblical categories of heart, soul, and mind.

Heart, soul, and mind constantly influence each other. The will or soul (Greek *psyche*, the root word for psychology) chooses what the conscious mind will dwell on. What the mind focuses on creates a track that it can follow with increasing ease, and these ideas eventually makes their way into the subconscious, which is part of the domain of the heart. The heart uses the input from the mind to form desires and attachments. These desires inform the will/soul, which then directs the mind to think even more about those desires. The heart can bypass the will to some extent (if we are not paying attention) and encourage the conscious mind directly to continue dwelling on the things it desires.

This dynamic explains the instructions in the Bible for dealing with our mental life. Phil. 4:8 tells us that we are to think about the things that are true, honorable, just, pure, lovely, commendable, excellent, and worthy of praise – implying that we should make a choice to do so rather than to allow our minds to just drift or to dwell on other things.

What we think about habitually shapes our hearts. Prov. 4:23 exhorts us to guard our heart, because from it flow the issues of life. The heart, the subconscious mind, is the seat of our deepest desires and is therefore the motivating force behind nearly everything we do. And we guard our heart by refusing to allow our minds to dwell on things that do not promote trust in God and by focusing on those that do (e.g., Phil. 4:6-7).

What all this means is that while we do have freedom to make choices, those choices are not random coin tosses—they are conditioned by our hearts' desires, "the weight of our love," as St. Augustine put it. Our ability to weigh options and make choices based on what we value enables us to prioritize, to decide how to use our time, to do meaningful work, to decide what to order at a restaurant. Most importantly, it also enables us to make moral choices.

For an action to be morally meaningful, it must be freely chosen. Many naturalists deny this connection, but the claim that our actions have moral significance is meaningless in the face of the naturalist's view that we are nothing more than biochemical machines. All our thoughts and actions are the products of physics and chemistry, making us little more than robots that have only the illusion of independent action. Under these circumstances, it is hard to make a credible claim that our actions are morally meaningful.[2]

---

[2] Considering the naturalist also rejects the idea that good and evil have any independent existence, it is unclear what "morally meaningful" would mean in a naturalist system.

The importance of moral freedom means that we must be able to choose to act either morally or immorally in any situation. Our choices, made by our will, are conditioned by the state of the heart and the "weight of our love." If we love goodness, we will choose the good. If we love something else more than goodness, we will choose that.

Our moral actions depend upon freedom, but that freedom in turn is governed by our hearts. This is why Jesus tells us that if we love Him, we will obey His commandments (Jn. 14:15, 21), as what we love determines our actions. The connection between what we love and our actions explains why Jesus said that the greatest commandment is to love God with all our heart, soul, mind, and strength, and the second to love our neighbor as ourselves (Matt. 22:37-40). Or as Paul puts it, love is the fulfillment of the Law (Rom. 13:10).

Beyond the personal level, we also see that God is concerned with freeing us from bondage of all kinds. The centerpiece of Israel's identity was God's freeing them from slavery in Egypt and leading them through the Exodus. This continued throughout the Bible and in the history of the Church. The Mosaic Law ordered that Israelite slaves be set free every seventh year; Jesus came to free us from our bondage to sin. The early Christians even went to Roman slave markets to purchase slaves for the specific purpose of setting them free. Freedom is a central element of the biblical story, and it is therefore not surprising that medieval theologians identified liberty as an inalienable right, given by God to all people and thus out of the reach of human authorities.

Human freedom is thus an important part of the Bible's message, and a critical element of the image of God. Unfortunately, the freedom to do good also means the freedom to choose the not-good instead. In the next chapter, we will explore what the choice not to do good means for the image of God that we bear.

Questions

1. Have you encountered anyone who denied free will? If so, on what basis did they do so? How do you respond to their arguments?

2. Why is freedom so important for carrying out our responsibilities as people created in the image of God? What are the different areas of life influenced by free will?

3. Lord Acton said, "Liberty is not the power of doing what we like, but the right of being able to do what we ought." Do you agree with him? Why or why not? Are there right and wrong uses of freedom?

4. By our free will, we can choose to do both positive and negative actions. We all want to do right, of course, but often we don't. When you are tempted and you fail, what kinds of considerations led you to choose to do wrong?

5. In his essay, "Men without Chests,"[3] C. S. Lewis talks about the battle between reason ("the head") and "mere appetites" ("the belly") in people. He argues that reason stands no chance in this battle without "the chest," which he describes as the seat of "emotions organized by *trained habit* into stable sentiments" (emphasis added). What can you do to develop the "trained habits" that build your "chest" so that you can control your appetites
6. and impulses?

7. Read John 8:31-36. How does knowing truth bring us freedom? What does sin do to our free will? Read Rom. 6:16-23. Which is true freedom, following our own desires even if they lead us to sin, or obeying Christ? Do you agree with Paul? What are the consequences of each choice?

EXTRA THOUGHTS
By Timothy D. Padgett

In the last few centuries, the quest for freedom has been so common in the West that it is hard to imagine a world where it did not matter as much as it does to us. But if we look back through time, and then toward a many societies today, we find that the presumption of human liberty has never been a sure thing. In fact, the idea of human rights as an essential feature of a moral culture is so rare

---

[3] http://www.columbia.edu/cu/augustine/arch/lewis/abolition1.htm.

that it could be called a novelty. So, where did it come from?

In the polytheistic world of ancient times, there was no reason to suppose that devotees of a rival god should be afforded equal treatment. In our own naturalist cosmology, the survival of the fittest is hardly a solid basis for the brotherhood of man. It was only in the biblical view of human nature (rooted in the image of God as a shared commodity among all human beings and all human groups) that freedom found its home. Each of us is equal before the only audience that matters. None of us can hold tightly the authority we possess over another.

Chapter 11

The Image of God and the Fall

When God created humanity, He gave us a tremendous privilege and responsibility to act as His stewards in the world, as well as amazing gifts to empower us to develop the Earth, create culture, and bring to completion the work that He began.

The Bible tells us in Gen. 2 that God placed Adam and Eve in the Garden of Eden and provided everything they needed to flourish: abundant food, close companionship, meaningful work, and an open relationship with Him. He placed only one restriction on them: they could not eat the fruit of the Tree of the Knowledge of Good and Evil (Gen. 2:17),[1] because on the day they did, they would die. Here was a test of obedience, self-restraint, trust, and love with clear consequences for disobedience.

---

[1] It was not an apple. That idea came from a Latin pun: the word for "evil" is *malus* and the word for "apple tree" is *mālus*. When the pun got translated into popular culture (and the vernacular), it was taken literally.

We failed comprehensively.

It started with the serpent persuading Eve to doubt God (Gen. 3:1-4). The "ice breaker" question was whether they could eat any fruit at all, to which Eve replied they could, except for the fruit of one tree—then she went beyond what God told her by saying they could not eat it or even touch it, or they would die.

Eve's first mistake was making a pharisaical misinterpretation of the commandment that prohibited more than was commanded. Then the serpent called God a liar outright and questioned His love and concern for Adam and Eve, suggesting that God was keeping something from them out of His own self-interest. Thus deceived, Eve began to think about the fruit – it was visually appealing and edible, the two key characteristics of the trees in the Garden, and so she decided to eat it. Not only that, but she gave some to Adam as well (Gen. 3:6).

Adam knew full well that what they were doing was wrong – he was not deceived by the serpent – but knowingly and intentionally decided to disobey anyway. John Milton's poem *Paradise Lost* suggests that Adam did this because he could not stand the thought of losing Eve, and thus completed the first sin that his wife had begun. Whatever his motive, however, Adam's action sealed the deal. They betrayed God first by lacking trust in His goodness and love, by doubting His word, by believing the deceiving serpent more than God, and finally by open rebellion.

The results were disastrous. The first and obvious one was shame (Gen. 3:7) and an effort to cover their sin by using creativity to fashion clothes of fig leaves. Their open relationship with God was broken, so they hid from Him out of shame and likely fear of consequences (Gen. 3:8). When God graciously sought them out and tried to coax a confession from them, sin shattered the unity that Adam and Eve enjoyed in their marriage. Adam put the blame on Eve *and on God Himself*: "the woman **you put here with me** gave me the fruit" (Gen. 3:12). For her part, Eve blamed the serpent (Gen. 3:13).

And so, God pronounced His judgment. The serpent was cursed to live in the dust, to unending hostility with Eve and her offspring, and ultimately to death at the hand of the "seed of the woman" (Gen. 3:14-15), a topic to which we will return in the next chapter.

Neither Eve nor Adam was cursed directly. For Eve, God's blessing was turned to a source of suffering. Prior to this, blessing was always associated with "being fruitful and multiplying"; now, Eve would experience pain in childbirth. Further, her relationship with Adam changed. Rather than the equality between the two that existed prior to this, Eve was now in the difficult position of "desiring" him – a reference to her sexuality and thus her inability to escape the first part of her judgment, as well as to her desire for the kind of psychological and emotional intimacy that had been lost – and also she became subordinated to him so that he would now "rule" over her the way they had together "ruled" over the other creatures (Gen. 3:16).[2] Instead of a gracious dance of husband and wife, their relationship would be corrupted by questions of power and manipulation. As a result, "the woman" (as she is known up to this point) is given a new name by Adam and only now becomes known as "Eve" (meaning "living"), since she would be the source of all subsequent human life (Gen. 3:20). Adam "naming" her may also be an indication of his "rule" over her after the Fall.

For Adam, the curse fell on the Earth itself. As God's steward, it was Adam's responsibility and privilege to "tend the Garden," growing his food and developing culture. What should have been a wonderful and joyful task would turn to drudgery. This strikes at the heart of what it meant to bear the image of God and to a critical element of man's identity. Just as Eve's role as the bearer of children was now filled with suffering, so the work necessary to fulfilling Adam's purpose became tainted with frustration and struggle. In fact, the word denoting "pain" is the same used to describe Eve's pain in childbirth and Adam's labor.

---

[2] This is not God's intent for marriage or a command about how things should be; it is a statement of what would follow. In the New Testament teaching about marriage, we see a restoration of much of the equality and mutuality that prevailed before the Fall.

Moreover, the prospect of death enters the picture, as God reminds Adam that he would return to the dust from which he had been taken (Gen. 3:17-19).

And so, in Gen. 3, we see sin breaking our fellowship with God, creating psychological problems within ourselves, striking at the heart of our families and our most intimate relationships, bringing pain into childbearing and struggle and frustration into our work, and even damaging our bodies. But all of this is only the tip of the iceberg. Sin affects every part of our being. It corrupts the desires of our hearts so that we do not want the things we should. Since our desires form our will, we choose to do wrong rather than right. Our corrupted hearts blind our reason and we refuse to see what is plain to us about God and the moral order (Rom. 1:18-32) and lead us to use our creativity to devise ways to do evil.[3] Like Eve, we do not trust God enough to obey Him, and like Adam, we openly defy Him.

Because of the sin of our primordial parents, we all have "original sin," that is, an inborn tendency to disobey God. To understand this, consider different breeds of dogs. Some are natural hunters and have behaviors bred into them that enhance their ability to do this well. Others are hopeless as hunters but amazing as herding dogs, again with different sets of behaviors they inherit from their ancestors. Just

---

[3] This is what Calvinists mean when they talk about "Total Depravity," not that we are as bad as we could be, but that every aspect of our being is affected by sin.

as dogs have been bred for specific behaviors, so are we. Only in our case, we have been bred to sin. Thus Seth, the progenitor of the *godly* line after the Fall, is described not as made in the image of God as Adam had been, but in the image of Adam (Gen. 5:2-3), indicating that Adam's sin was passed down to him.

But the problem of sin is even bigger than that. Since we are made in the image of God and are His regents on earth, our human sin has affected even the natural world so that it cannot fulfill the purposes which God intended for it (Rom. 8:20-22). Our failure means that God's intent for the world to be developed, for the Garden of Eden to become the City of God, was delayed and even threatened.

But God's will cannot be thwarted. Even though Adam's offspring bore his fallen and sinful image, the image of God was not lost—it was marred, but it was not completely effaced. After the Flood, God affirmed to Noah that human beings were all made in His image (Gen. 9:6). We remain God's regents here, even though it is a much more painful and difficult job to do so since we must fight not only the cursed ground but our own nature as well.

Further, God had His plans in place for Adam's disobedience. Though Adam was reminded of his mortality, he did not die on the day he ate the fruit. Something else did. God Himself replaced the fig leaves with clothes made from animal skins for Adam and Eve (Gen. 3:21). Our parents' guilt and shame were covered by an animal that died so they would not have to. A substitutionary sacrifice for their sin that pointed the way to a time that the Seed of the woman would destroy the serpent but be wounded Himself in the process (Gen. 3:17). We will examine that in more detail in our next chapter.

Questions

1. This chapter argues that you cannot have virtue without the potential for vice, and thus free will automatically creates the potential for evil. Do you agree? Why or why not? What is the difference between that statement and the idea that you cannot have good without evil?

2. Read Rom. 5:12-14. According to this passage, what is the relationship between Adam's sin and our own? Original sin is a very controversial idea in some circles. Does this passage support the idea of original sin? Why or why not?

3. How much of an effect does sin have within us? Does it influence all parts of our being, as Calvinists teach?

4. Trappist monk Thomas Merton wrote, "One of the effects of original sin is an instinctive prejudice in favour of our own selfish desires. We see things as they are not, because we see them centered on ourselves. Fear, anxiety, greed, ambition and our hopeless need for pleasure all distort the image of reality that is reflected in our minds." Where do you see people distorting reality in favor of their own preferred view of the world? Can you identify any ways in which you do this yourself?

5. People frequently argue that crime is caused by poverty, social conditions, or other unfavorable circumstances in life. What does the story of the Fall in Genesis 3 suggest about these explanations of crime? What do you think causes criminal behavior?

6. Can we be good without God? Why or why not?

EXTRA THOUGHTS
By Timothy D. Padgett

One of the most encouraging aspects of the Christian worldview is that the world is not the way it is supposed to be. At first glance, this seems like nonsense. How on earth can it be a positive development that things have gone drastically off course? In its most obvious sense, the Fall is the worst news of all. God's good creation has been warped and twisted into a disgusting facsimile of the beauty He had originally wrought.

However, if the world was as it is without a Fall drawing it down, then all the wickedness around us would be "normal." The suffering we experienced would not be odd to us. The doctrine of the Fall gives words to what our hearts tell us: that there is something rotten in the state of humanity, that oppression and tyranny, disease, and death are things we were never designed to see. The evil we see inflicted on our neighbors and ourselves is not just "different" or a mistake; it is a violation of the high point of creation—the image of God in each human life.

Chapter 12

The Image of God and Jesus the Christ

Adam and Eve's fall into sin had immediate and devastating effects on their relationship with God (hiding and separation), with each other (blame and recrimination), and with themselves (shame and guilt). The judgment which followed struck at the heart of God's blessing to them (pain in childbirth) and of His mandate to tend the garden and develop culture (pain in work). It also made this a lifelong sentence, ending only in death.[1] Nonetheless, Adam and Eve were not relieved of their responsibility as God's stewards. They and their descendants continued to be God's image-bearers. Now, however, their job would be infinitely harder.

In the devastation brought about by sin and judgment, however, we have a word of hope. God told the serpent: "I

---

[1] This is one reason Adam and Eve were expelled from the Garden: to keep them from eating from the Tree of Life and never dying. In a world of suffering and change, natural death and an end to toil and pain can be a mercy.

will put enmity between you and the woman, and between your seed and her seed. And he shall bruise your head and you shall bruise his heel" (Gen. 3:15). This promise, known as the *protoevangelium* ("first Gospel"), points to a day when the "seed of the woman" would deliver a fatal blow to the serpent but would Himself be wounded in the process.

Over the course of the Old Testament scriptures, the seed of the woman would be narrowed down to the seed of Abraham, of Isaac, of Jacob, of Judah, and of David. We learn in Isaiah that the promise would be fulfilled by the child of a virgin, who would be God with us. Ultimately, these promises and prophecies were fulfilled in Jesus, the child of a virgin mother, "who was descended from David according to the flesh and was declared to be the Son of God in power according to the Spirit of holiness…." (Rom 1:3b-4a).

God gave Adam and Eve real agency, allowing them the risk of disobeying His commands and throwing the world into chaos. But the chaos would not win. After their sin, God put in motion a plan He had in place even from before the foundation of the world (cf. Rev. 13:8). The scope of that plan is nothing short of breathtaking.

First, Jesus dealt with our guilt. God had told Adam that on the day he ate the fruit of the Tree of the Knowledge of Good and Evil, he would die. Spiritually, he did die, but not physically. God provided a substitute, an animal that

The Image of God and Jesus the Christ 117

died to provide the skins that would cover Adam and Eve's shame. Here we have the first substitutionary sacrifice, pointing ahead to the sacrificial system of the Law and ultimately to Jesus' death on the cross, whereby he delivered the death blow to Satan and was wounded in the process. All the earlier sacrifices, from Eden onwards, were pictures of the coming sacrifice of Jesus, whose death finally and definitively paid in full the debt we owe to God for our disobedience.

For Jesus' death to be effective, however, He needed to be sinless Himself. For that He needed, like Adam, to be born without the taint of original sin dragging Him down.[2] He had to be, in essence, a new Adam; one who faced the testing of His obedience but unlike the first Adam, remained faithful in that testing. He also experienced the full brunt of suffering in this world and God's judgment on Adam – He worked as a skilled craftsman; he experienced hunger, thirst, and exhaustion. He was misunderstood and slandered, rejected, betrayed by those closest to Him, mocked, tortured, and killed. But through it all, He never lost His trust in God and never wavered in His obedience and submission to God's will.

He then rose from the dead, His transformed body becoming a paradigm for the bodies His followers will

---

[2] This probably has something to do with the virgin birth, though how exactly sin is transmitted is not explained in Scripture.

receive at the resurrection. But even in this world, the resurrection matters: Jesus' death broke the hold of sin and death over our lives, and the resurrection then gives us new life and the power to live in obedience to God's calling. We participate in the great exchange – Jesus takes our guilt, and we take His righteousness; Jesus takes our punishment, and we receive His reward; Jesus suffers death for us, and we receive His life in this world and the next.

All this is predicated on faith and trust – the very site where Adam and Eve failed. In essence, we get what we place our trust in. If we trust Christ, we receive what He deserves; if we trust in ourselves, we get what we deserve. If we trust in Christ, we get His power to live the way we were made to live; if we trust ourselves, we are on our own.

So, Jesus is truly the new Adam (1 Cor. 15:45, cf. Rom. 5:12-21), the progenitor of a new humanity redeemed from guilt, delivered from death, and empowered to carry out God's mission and purposes in this world.

There is still more. Col. 1:15 tells us that Jesus "... is the image of the invisible God, the firstborn of all creation." Humanity was made in the image of God and continues to bear it, but Jesus is preeminently the image of God, the one who is God's definitive representative on Earth, who speaks with God's voice and authority, who is quite literally the face of God on Earth—the fullness of deity in bodily form (vs. 19).

As the firstborn[3] of creation, Jesus is the heir of all things, the means by which everything came into existence and the one who holds everything together, as Col. 1:15-20 explains. This makes him preeminent over the created order, the one who fully exercises the dominion given to humanity. Salvation is thus truly cosmic in scope: John 3:16 tells us that God loved the *cosmos*, the ordered world that was subject to futility because of human sin (Rom. 8:20). Just as the bodies of the redeemed will be transformed at the resurrection, so will the creation as God brings forth a new heavens and Earth where righteousness dwells (1 Pet. 3:13).

Until then, we are living in a new reality in this world. Sin may have marred the image of God and made our mandate to "tend and keep the Garden" under God's authority far more difficult, but in Christ the power of sin over our lives has been broken. We are thus freer than we have been since Adam to fulfill God's original calling to humanity, to act as His stewards in all that we do in the world. Our redemption in Christ restores to us the ability to fulfill the cultural mandate that God gave to Adam yet never revoked. As we carry out the Great Commission and make disciples for Christ (the image of God and our sovereign king), we are to call people not just to Heaven, but to live out the Lordship

---

[3]"Firstborn" is not always literal in Scripture; it also refers to someone who is an heir (whether the firstborn or not) or someone who is preeminent in some way. Given the following verses, it is clear that Paul is not describing Jesus as the first created being but rather as the one who is preeminent over all creation, including the spiritual world.

of Christ in every area of their lives. By this we fulfill our original calling on Earth.

Questions

1. What is your understanding of the Gospel? Is it just about forgiveness of sins, or is it more than that?

2. What does it mean that Christ is the "new Adam"? How does he fulfill the role of the first Adam? Review the discussion of the image of God in the previous chapters. How does Jesus fulfill the different facets we've examined?

3. Why is Jesus' resurrection important? What affect does it have on our lives today? In the future?

4. Read Col. 1:15-20.] Besides our salvation, what does this passage teach you about Jesus' work?

5. In the hymn "Joy to the World," Isaac Watts wrote:

    No more let sins and sorrows grow
    Nor thorns infest the ground.
    He comes to make His blessings flow
    Far as the curse is found.

    Do you see the work of Christ as extending "far as the curse is found"? How far does the curse extend? How does the work of Christ reach to all of those areas?

6. When you think of Jesus, how do you picture him? Read Rev. 1:13-18. How does this affect how you think of Jesus?

EXTRA THOUGHTS
By William E. Brown, Senior Fellow for Worldview and Culture

Two thoughts about Jesus and the image of God: First, *Jesus was fully human and thus created in the image of God*. The Gospel accounts of the birth and life of Jesus teach and display His full humanity. He was physically born and physically died. He felt human emotions—He wept, He loved, He got angry. He experienced human limitations—He was hungry, thirsty, and weary. Since all humans are created in God's image, then so was Jesus.

Second, *Jesus is in the image of God because He is God*. Setting aside His authoritative teaching and miracles (which would be sufficient to make a case for His deity), even His enemies recognized Jesus was "making himself equal with God" (John 5:18). He confirmed to His disciples that "I and the Father are one" (John 10:30). When the disciple Philip requested that He show them the Father, Jesus replied, "Whoever has seen me has seen the Father. How can you say, 'Show us the Father?'" (John 14:8-9).

Jesus Christ: fully human and fully God. He is the man in whom "the whole fullness of deity dwells bodily" (Colossians 2:9).

Chapter 13

The Image of God and Restoration

The fall into sin had devastating effects on Adam and Eve, as a direct consequence of their disobedience, and in the judgment from God that followed. We see in Gen. 3 sin producing alienation from God as Adam and Eve hid from Him, from ourselves with feelings of shame, from our neighbor with Adam blaming Eve and the distortion of their relationship as husband, and ultimately from the natural world as the ground resists rather than yielding its bounty to Adam's labor.

Given the breadth of the effects of sin, God's plan of restoration had to to deal comprehensively with all of these problems. Redemption in Christ is much bigger than simply dealing with the guilt of our sin and restoring our relationship with God, as important as that is. Redemption provides the means for dealing with the consequences of the Fall in this life.

Psychologically, many (though by no means all) of our problems stem from guilt – on this, at least, Sigmund Freud had a valid point, though he failed to recognize that guilt is not simply a matter of feelings in our minds. Rather, true moral guilt exists and is the source of many of our guilty feelings. Pop psychology has followed Freud in denying the reality of guilt and trying to free people from *feeling* guilty without ever addressing or even recognizing the underlying problem of our guilt. Because pop psychology has no means of dealing with true guilt, it can never fully solve our psychological problems.

The good news is that in Christ, our guilt is taken away. What He has done on the cross means we no longer need to hide from guilt or deny it. In fact we now acknowledge and confess it, agreeing with God about His evaluation of our behavior, but also trusting in Christ to bear our guilt and shame. This is a firm foundation to deal with our true guilt as well as our feelings of guilt, and shame at our behavior. God knows all about it, and He has accepted and forgiven us anyway. While we need to mourn our sin and repent of it, we need not allow it to paralyze us anymore.

Christianity also did much to restore relationships between people who were often hostile to each other. Early Christians insisted that all people were spiritually and morally equal before God. This led to a vastly different ethic among early Christians from the traditional one. The ethic is in keeping with Jesus' commands to love our enemies and pray for those who persecute us (Matt. 5:44), to love our neighbors as ourselves (Matt. 22:39). Paul expands upon it by teaching about humility (Phil. 2:1-4), and about Christ demolishing the dividing wall of hostility between Jews and Gentiles (Eph. 2:14).

The historical consequences of this new view of our equality before God in Christ steered Christians to lead the battle to eliminate slavery. The starting point was during the Roman Empire as churches and individual Christians purchased slaves for the sole purpose of setting them free. The same beliefs led Christians to oppose abortion and infanticide and led the monk Telemachus to try to halt a gladiatorial match, even at the cost of his own life. Modern ideas of civil equality and human rights also have their roots in Christian thought.

In particular, the Christian emphasis on spiritual and moral equality led to a new view of women and a restoration of marriage as a partnership between fellow image bearers. As we have seen, the Woman was made as an equal of the Man, though it seems that the Man was to be the leader in the relationship (as indicated by his naming the Woman in Gen. 2:23). This proper relationship was distorted by the Fall, with the subjugation of women following as the result of sin. This type of subjugation was a central element of Greco-Roman culture, as was pervasive misogyny.

In contrast, Paul taught that we are all to be subject to each other for the love of Christ: wives are subject to husbands, and husbands are to love their wives as Christ loved us: He looked out for our interests rather than His own and laid down His life for us (Eph. 5:21-33). The role of the husband is thus transformed into a servant-leader who has no right to insist on his way but who must self-sacrificially serve his wife.[1] This new attitude also gave women new rights and status within Christian communities, as documented by Rodney Stark.[2]

The coming of Christ also begins the process of restoring the harmony of the natural world, as prophesied in the peaceful kingdom passage (Is. 11:6-9) and in promises of the desert blooming and flowing with water (Is. 35:1-2, 6-7). The full restoration of Creation to its proper functioning awaits the Second Coming. In the meantime Christians have historically called for responsible stewardship of resources on the one hand, and have worked to mitigate the effects of the Fall on our labor on the other.

As we have seen, God intended work to be good and fulfilling, but sin turned it into drudgery. Not surprisingly, then, in the ancient world across the globe, labor was seen

---

[1] See the earlier articles in this series on gender (http://www.colsoncenter.org/the-center/columns/call-response/15392-the-image-of-god-and-gender) and marriage (http://www.colsoncenter.org/the-center/columns/call-response/15458-the-image-of-god-and-marriage).

[2] See *The Rise of Christianity*, 95-128.

as something fit only for slaves and supposed inferiors. In Christianity, work was restored to an honored place. Paul himself worked (Acts 18:3) and encouraged others to do so (1 Thes. 4:11; 2 Thes. 3:10). For this very reason, early monks were commanded to engage in work, both as an exercise in humility and out of obedience to biblical principles.

But if labor is good, then mere drudgery is evil. People should work, but they should do so in a way that engages the whole person as much as possible. People should not be bound to repetitive, mindless tasks that animals or machines can do just as well. This undermines the intrinsic dignity of work. To alleviate this tension historically, monasteries of the Middle Ages began an early industrial revolution, harnessing water power to grind grain. The technology was then adapted to make cloth, operate bellows in foundries and trip hammers in forges, and make paper, among many other tasks. Wind power was similarly harnessed for the same tasks as well as for pumping water out of the polders in the Netherlands (land reclaimed from the sea for farming).

A host of other technologies developed in the Christian Middle Ages, ranging from eyeglasses to blast furnaces, horseshoes to spinning wheels. The effort to produce technologies to improve work and working-class life has continued in the West ever since.

Other cultures had fabulous technologies long before the West began to develop. The difference is that those technologies were never used to develop labor saving devices or to benefit the working class. The Romans, for example, knew about water wheels but never deployed them because they had slaves to do work.

The difference was worldview. Christians recognized the dignity of work and the equal dignity between humans. This alone, provided the motivation for harnessing technology to benefit workers, not just elites, and in the process laid the economic foundation for the rise of the West.

On another front, Christians developed the scientific method and were at the heart of the scientific revolution because they recognized the divine mandate to study the world (chapter 9) and knew that the world was made by a rational God and must therefore be rational itself. Learning about the world meant studying it as it is, because only through that would the mind of God be revealed.

The examples of the impact of Christianity are numerous. All, without exception, depend entirely on the work of Christ for their effectiveness. Without the reconciling work of Christ on the cross, we have no basis for psychological healing, for overcoming the differences of race, ethnicity, class, or gender, no power to carry out the mandate God gave us in Adam, and no means of overcoming the curse that our sin laid upon us. But in Christ, all is possible. As

Christians, our part is to continue Christ's work in reversing the curse, working to reconcile our neighbors with God and to bring the blessings of His rule into all areas of life.

Questions

1. What aspects of the work of Christ discussed here are new to you or are things you have not spent much time considering? Which do you usually hear about or read about?

2. Given the fact that everyone sins, how do you handle your guilt? How do you handle the guilt of people who wrong you or those close to you? How does Christ's death on the cross affect your response to guilt, including that of those who hurt you?

3. Is there such a thing as universal human rights? If so, where do they come from? How do the truths of the Bible contribute to our understanding of human rights?

4. Read John 17:20-26. What was on Jesus' mind as he was heading into the crucifixion? How have you seen Jesus' work reconcile people across lines that normally divide them—race, class, languages, etc.?

5. Dutch theologian Abraham Kuyper once said, "...there is not a square inch in the whole domain of our human existence over which Christ, who is Sovereign over all, does not cry: "Mine!"" If that is true, what does Christ's sovereignty mean for your job? How does the work of Christ affect your work?

6. Read Rom. 8:19-22. What does it mean that the creation was subject to futility? What does this tell you about the scope of Christ's redemption?

EXTRA THOUGHTS
By Timothy D. Padgett

Breaking news! The Book of Revelation is confusing. The same goes for the rest of the Bible's apocalyptic literature, whether we are talking about Daniel's statues and beasts or Zechariah's flying scroll. Debate about its meaning has gone on for centuries, and there is little chance that this will change in the future. Do you want to know a secret? The meaning is simple. Simple enough, in fact, that the point of Revelation can be shown in two words: God wins. Despite the hatred of His enemies, He will restore the glory of His creation.

When we talk about restoration and the image of God, we must bear in mind that this restoration extends to the created goodness of our human nature. When Christ restores His world by "making all things new," He is not looking to undo the wonder of Eden's beauty, nor will He strip away the glory of what He made humanity to be for the sake of a bloodless future. Our passions, our creativity, our curiosities, and even our physicality—all of these are part of what He crafted when He drew Adam from the dirt. The restoration which God has planned involves our becoming more, not less, human.

Chapter 14

The Image of God and the Cultural Mandate

To understand fully God's intentions for Christians in this world, we need to grasp what it means that we are made in the image of God. As we have seen in earlier chapters, the term "image of a god" in the ancient Near East referred to someone who was a representative or regent of that god. For us, it means that our primary identity as human beings is as God's stewards over the world He has made. In a broad sense, it also includes the gifts and abilities God has placed in us that enable us to carry out this work, including gender and marriage, spirituality and physicality, creativity, rationality, freedom, and morality.

Our call as stewards is to continue the work which God has begun. He started with a world "without form and void" and set it in proper order. We are to "tend the Garden," including both the cultivation of beauty through the arts as well as the production of food and other necessities. We are also to engage in the processes of learning and discovery by coming to understand the natural world, and we are to do all of this in obedience to God. We recognize His authority over the world to cultivate it as stewards, not owners, and do not abuse His property.

The reality, however, is that we abuse our authority. The story of the Fall points out that we were not willing to live within the limits God placed on us. The result was broken relationships with God, with each other, with ourselves, and with nature itself. The blessing of children becomes a source of suffering for women, and the blessing of work becomes a source of suffering and frustration for men. Yet the curse on Adam nor Eve was not absolute. Children continue to be a blessing, and our call as God's regents in the world was never withdrawn. We continue to be God's image and His face in the world, even in the midst of our persistent rebellion.

In the face of this sin, God had a recovery plan for our disobedience. Through the incarnation of Jesus Christ, the ultimate image of God, through His death, resurrection, and ascension, the penalty due to our sin is paid in full and the power of sin in our lives is broken, thus restoring our relationship with God. This is the foundation for reconciliation with each other, and for dealing with the problem of guilt and shame in our lives. But our redemption in Christ also restores our work and purpose to its proper place. Under the influence of the biblical worldview, the Western world developed technologies to eliminate

The Image of God and the Cultural Mandate

drudgery and to enhance productivity, making Western cultures the most prosperous in human history—with both good and bad consequences because of the lingering effect of sin.

What shall we say in response to this?

To put this differently, in Christ our ability to live out our call as the image of God is restored. Sin is not gone, but it does not have the same hold over us. We are now free to carry out our mandate to develop culture as stewards of God. This has enormous implications for how we live our lives.

First, it means that Christianity is far more than what most people – including most Christians – think of as "religion." Too typically, Christianity is understood as little more than religious activities plus morality). Rather, Christianity is a worldview, a vision of the world and our place in it where every facet of our life – family, occupation, recreation, relationships, finances, *everything* – finds its meaning and end in God's purposes for us and for the world. The Gospel affects all of life and includes the stewardship of all that God has entrusted to us, whether time, talents, treasure, or relationships.

Second, we need to be active in every sphere of life and should infuse everything we do with the sure knowledge that we are fulfilling God's call on our lives to be stewards wherever we are. While we need to work from the foundation provided by Christ's redemption, we do not necessarily need to wear this on our sleeves. C. S. Lewis once commented that "we don't need more Christian writers, we need more great writers who are Christian." The point here is that not everything we do needs to be overtly "Christian." Instead, we need to do whatever we do with excellence, because by so doing we are being good and faithful servants in fulfilling God's purposes for the world. This is what it means that we are to do everything as unto God, not man, and to do it in the name of Christ.

Third, we need to get rid of the idea that only clergy are involved in "full-time Christian service." When we understand that all of culture is under God's authority and that He equips each of us to follow our unique calling, it is clear that all work be considered Christian service. Christians in the "secular" sphere are fulfilling God's call to be His stewards by developing culture. To be sure, some are called to vocational ministry as members of the clergy, but their work is no more or less sacred than the business owner or laborer whose work is a calling from God.

Fourth, although evangelism is critically important, it is only the first step for Christians. The Great Commission tells us that wherever we go,[1] we are to make disciples who

---

[1] The word "go" in the Greek is not a command, it is a participle. The sense is more "in your going" or "as you go" rather than a command to go.

obey everything that Jesus taught. In other words, we are to make obedient disciples, not just converts. Evangelism must lead to discipleship, to teaching people how to live for Jesus in their own walks of life.

Jesus called only twelve to be apostles. He left his other disciples in their own professions. We must learn what it means to be a Christian in our own calling and to help others learn what it means in theirs, not only in our employment, but in our family, neighborhood, community, and nation, in our friendships, our recreation, even in the care of ourselves. And for this, we need the support and fellowship of other Christians, our fellow members of the body of Christ.

Lastly, to do all of this, we need to catch a vision of why we matter. John Calvin said that the entire universe is "the theater of God's glory," and yet in this amazing, mysterious, and beautiful universe we occupy a unique place. We alone bridge the gap between time and eternity, matter, and spirit, and we have a particular calling to bring to fruition the things God has begun. Each of us is designed and equipped to play a key part that only we can do to bring about God's purposes for His creation. God saved us when we could not save ourselves so that we would carry out the work that He uniquely prepared us to do (Eph. 2:8-10). John 3:16 tells us that God loved the *world* (Greek *cosmos*, the entirety of creation) so much that He gave His son to save those who believe in Him. Our salvation is thus not only for ourselves personally, but for the good of the entire created order.

With all this in mind, let us take up the challenge to live out our identity as God's image on Earth, bringing the lordship of Christ to bear in all areas of life, and recognizing our unique and critical role, however small it may look to us, in fulfilling God's purposes for the world. And whatever we do, whether in word or deed, let us do it as unto God, not men, in the name of our Lord Jesus Christ.

Questions

1. This chapter argues that Christians are called and equipped not only to save the lost, but to bring them into the kingdom where we can work together to complete the task God originally gave to Adam in the Garden to build culture. Is this a common view in your Christian circles, or is this a new idea to you? Do you agree or disagree with this understanding of the Gospel? Why?

2. Read Matt. 28:18-20. Has anyone taught you to be a disciple who obeys everything that Jesus taught? Is this something you are doing with others? Is this something your church actively promotes? What can you do to help others to grow as obedient disciples?

3. Make a list of all your roles, relationships, and activities. How central is the lordship of Christ to each of these? Where can you go for help in the areas where you are weak?

4. Modern society has bought into the idea of a division between the sacred and the secular. For the Christian, should there be?

How much of this division do you see in your own thinking, in the approach to Christianity in your church, and among your Christian friends?

5. Why is it important to do all our work, whether obviously "Christian" or not, with excellence?

6. What are the most important lessons you have learned from this study of the image of God? What concrete steps will you take to incorporate these lessons into your life?

EXTRA THOUGHTS
By Maria Baer, Senior Writer and Podcast Cohost

What *is* "work" exactly? God's cultural mandate to His creation means our labors are so much more than merely the times we punch a clock or even just a financial proposition. Reducing our concept of "real work" to this is a mistake. First, it supposes that those who are "out of" that kind of work have nothing to offer in terms of building culture. Second, it minimizes the great meaning of the hours we do spend behind a desk or in a factory or building houses or answering phones.

Our lives build culture whether we mean them to or not. God's cultural mandate is His beckoning to us to make culture on purpose—to do *good work*, at home, in our families, in our relationships, and even in our quiet moments alone. We build His kingdom and steward His creation every time we serve others, worship Him, and follow His calling from moment to moment. And if we do not think our "work" really matters, we run the risk of building a different kingdom. One full of moths and rust that will not last much beyond the time we punch out.